THE DIRT CHEAP GREEN THUMB

The mission of Storey Publishing is to serve our customers by
publishing practical information that encourages
personal independence in harmony with the environment.

Edited by Gwen Steege and Lisa H. Hiley
Art direction and book design by Dan O. Williams
How-to illustrations by Brigita Fuhrmann, except for pages 42, 68, 112, 113,
    117, 170 (2nd from top), 190, 225, 251 by Alison Kolesar, and 196 and 214
    by © Elayne Sears
Decorative illustrations and typography by Dan O. Williams
Expert read by Anne Halpin White
Indexed by Nancy D. Wood

The Dirt-Cheap Green Thumb is a revised and expanded edition of *Dirt-Cheap Gardening*,
    Storey Communications, 1994

Storey books are available for special premium and promotional uses and for customized
editions. For further information, please call 1-800-793-9396.

Storey Publishing
210 MASS MoCA Way
North Adams, MA 01247
www.storey.com

Printed in the United States by Versa Press
10 9 8 7 6 5 4 3 2 1

Library of Congress Cataloging-in-Publication Data
Massingham, Rhonda, 1959–
  The dirt-cheap green thumb / Rhonda Massingham Hart. — [2nd ed.]
    p. cm.
  First ed. published as: Dirt cheap gardening.
  Includes index.
  ISBN 978-1-60342-441-7 (pbk. : alk. paper) 1. Gardening.
  I. Title. II. Title: Dirt cheap green thumb.
SB453.M375 2009
635—dc22

                    2009023716

THE DIRT CHEAP

400 THRIFTY TIPS
FOR SAVING MONEY, TIME, AND RESOURCES
AS YOU GARDEN

GREEN THUMB

RHONDA MASSINGHAM HART

Storey Publishing

To my father, Richard Massingham,
With love and gratitude.
Thanks, Dad.

Acknowledgments

In large part, the first edition of this book was made possible by the Washington State University, Spokane County Extension Master Gardener's Program. Thanks also to Nancy Cashon, Scott McLaughlin, and Chris Culbertson for their help in pulling together the first edition.

Special thanks for the kind and always welcome suggestions of Gwen Steege at Storey, without whom there would have been no second edition. Thanks seem insufficient for the tireless and cheerful contributions of my editor, Lisa Hiley, and copy editor, Eileen Clawson, who helped transform my jumble of words into actual sentences, and to the designer, Dan Williams, who made it all come to life, but thank you!

And finally, thanks to fellow gardener, writer, and penny-pincher, Mark McKinnon, for the inspiration to stay on track.

Here's to dirty fingernails!

Contents

THE DIRT ON CHEAP GARDENING vi

1: THE ABSOLUTES 1

2: TOOLS VERSUS TOYS 47

3: PRICELESS PLANTS 79

4: WINNING VARIETIES 108

5: SAVE FROM THE START 120

6: PLANT WELLNESS PAYS 139

7: CHEAP SKILLS 181

8: LANDSCAPE FOR LESS 202

**9: LONGER LIFE FOR YOUR PLANT
   DOLLARS** 220

10: REAP BOUNTIFUL HARVESTS 232

APPENDIXES

A: Recommended Disease-Resistant Varieties 256

B: Money-Saving Vegetable Varieties 261

C: High-Productivity Fruit Varieties 267

RESOURCES 269

INDEX 277

Introduction

The Dirt on Cheap Gardening

I've always been a little confused by references to "lazy gardeners," because I don't know any. Gardeners seem compelled to work. Those green thumbs make our hands restless.

These days, especially, there is another common thread among gardeners — the desire to save money. Whether it's growing your own food or simply mowing your own lawn, there are lots of ways getting down and dirty will save you money. Not to mention, make you healthier.

The Dirt-Cheap Green Thumb is for frugal people, whether you're a well-established gardener or a beginner. Filled with hundreds of tips on everything from acquiring seed and plants to harvesting your crops, the aim of this book is to help you cut costs. Some of the savings are minor. For instance, seed is still a bargain compared to other garden expenses. Some savings are major, such as tips on saving hundreds, if not thousands, of dollars on equipment. But they all add up, and most carry benefits above and beyond the dollar savings. Many of the tips also are time-saving ideas. Even though I am cheap, or frugal, I know that nothing is more valuable than your time.

And don't think for a minute that an inexpensive garden has to look cheap. All it takes is a little time, energy, and creativity — without a lot of money — to have a garden others will envy.

Rhonda Massingham Hart

CHAPTER 1

THE ABSOLUTES

What elements do you really *need* to start a garden? The simple requirements are soil, sun, water, and seed. But what about location of the soil, the *type* of soil, and its structure and content? How much sun is enough, and can you enhance exposure? How much water is necessary, and how will you deliver it? How will you choose the right seeds? Do you even *want* seeds, or should you buy transplants instead? Like I said, it's simple!

The Perfect Garden

Let's begin with the first choice every budding gardener must make: the site of the garden. Whether you are landscaping a small city plot or planting a large country garden, you must take stock of your site first. Imagine what you'd do if you could choose the perfect garden site. It would include the following:

▶ **A gentle south-facing slope.** Southern exposure maximizes sunlight, and a slight slope facilitates water drainage and air circulation.

▶ **Well-draining soil.** Soil should stay moist but not soggy.

▶ **Fertile, friable loam.** Good soil is rich in microbes and organic matter. Nobody ever just finds soil like this; it takes years of building.

▶ **Full sun.** Many plants prefer it, and you can surround those that don't with trees, shrubs, or garden structures.

▶ **Available water.** Realistically, how far are you willing to lug the garden hose?

Your Actual Garden

Unfortunately, most of us don't have the luxury of choosing exactly the right garden site. We have a yard, and the garden goes there. Even the smallest yard, however, has a variety of growing areas within it, known as microclimates. All plants have their own unique growing requirements. Some plants thrive in a shaded spot, while others falter there for lack of sunlight. When assessing your site, take note of your microclimates. They will help you decide what plants to grow and where to put them.

DIRT CHEAP

Why should the cash-conscious gardener care about microclimates? Because if you plant things where they don't like to grow, you waste money, time, and effort. Look carefully at the microclimates surrounding your house so you can select plants that are best suited to grow in each area.

Maximizing Microclimates

To understand microclimates a little better, let's look at a typical house and yard, as illustrated. The north side of the house is shady from midmorning through the end of the day. The east side receives morning sun but not direct sun in the afternoon. The south side's yard receives full sun all day long. And the west side of the house doesn't get full sun until midday but then bakes until dusk.

Each side of the house has a different set of growing conditions and is a distinct microclimate. Landscaping will create even more microclimates. A white-painted fence along the yard, a pond, trees, and bushes will produce different growing conditions for plants near them.

Test soil drainage by digging 18-inch-deep holes in various locations around your garden and filling them with water. After they have drained completely, fill again and check hourly. If it takes three hours or less to drain, you may have more sand in your soil than is optimal. Four to six hours is ideal; more than that means your soil drainage may need some improvement.

GREEN THUMB

Make the most of your site by finding out about the **average rainfall** for your area; the **average first and last frost dates,** from which you can then calculate your anticipated growing season; the **low temperatures** in your area and your USDA Zone designation; and the **pH of your soil.**

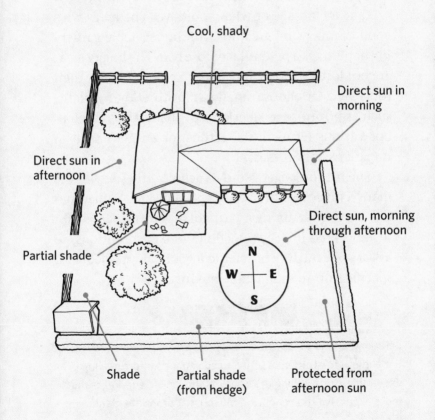

Cool, shady

Direct sun in morning

Direct sun in afternoon

Direct sun, morning through afternoon

Partial shade

N
W — E
S

Shade

Partial shade (from hedge)

Protected from afternoon sun

Work with Your Site

Chances are that your yard fulfills at least some of the specifications for the perfect garden site. It may have adequate drainage, except for one corner; full sun in many spots; and conveniently located water.

Take advantage of what you have. The areas with good drainage are great for fruit or vegetable gardening or perhaps a perennial or rose bed. The boggy areas are not lost—willows and alder trees love having their roots wet. Or choose smaller, moisture-loving plants such as primrose or Siberian iris. Shady areas can harbor various ferns, hosta, astilbe, or annuals such as impatiens or begonias.

The lists on pages 7 and 8 include only some of the many choices you have for specific sites. Sometimes not all the plants in a particular genus (maples, for instance) require the same light or soil conditions, so ask at your nursery or refer to a good encyclopedia for specific information before buying.

DIRT CHEAP

Selecting plants for specific sites will save you dollars, hours, and the endless frustration of trying to coax plants into surviving in an unsuitable site. Keeping the wrong plants on life support is much more expensive than choosing the most appropriate plant in the first place.

Plants That Like Full Sun

Annuals/Biennials
Ageratum*
Alyssum, sweet**
Calendula
Celosia
Chamomile
Cosmos
Dianthus
Herbs (many)
Marigold
Nasturtium
Petunia
Portulaca
Salvia
Vegetables
Zinnia

Perennials
Aster
Blanket flower
Candytuft
Clematis
Columbine*
Coralbell**
Coreopsis
Creeping thyme
Crocus
Daffodil*
Daisy*
Daylily
Grasses, ornamental
Iris
Lady's mantle*

Peony
Phlox, garden
Purple
  coneflower
Rudbeckia
Sedum*
Sunflower
Sweet pea
Tulip
Violet*
Virginia creeper
Yarrow
Yucca

*Tolerates some shade
**Prefers partial shade in hot areas

Trees/Shrubs
Blue mist
Cotoneaster
Flowering quince
Forsythia
Fruit trees (most)
Junipers
Larch/tamarack

Lilac
Mock orange
Oaks (most)
Pines (most)
Potentilla
Rose of Sharon
Roses

Spiraea
Staghorn sumac
Tree peony
Tulip tree
Walnut
Weigela

Plants That Like Shade

Annuals/Biennials

Begonia	Foxglove	Sweet William
Coleus	Impatiens	Viola/pansy
Flowering tobacco	Lobelia	Wishbone flower

Perennials

Astilbe*	Geranium, hardy	Primrose
Bleeding heart	Hellebore	Sweet woodruff
Bugleweed	Hosta	Trillium
Corydalis, yellow	Lily-of-the-valley	Vinca minor*
Ferns, various	Pachysandra	

*Tolerates full sun in the North

Trees/Shrubs

Azalea	Fothergilla	Rhododendron
Blueberry	Fuchsia	Serviceberry
Boxwood	Hemlock	Viburnum
Camellia	Mountain laurel	
Dogwood	Oregon grape	

Plants That Like Moist Soil

Perennials

Astilbe	Dichondra
Bergenia	Iris
Calla	Mint
Cattail	Mosses (some)
Daylily	Primrose

Trees/Shrubs

American cranberry	Red maple
American holly	Red osier dogwood
Chokeberry	River birch
Elderberry	Serviceberry
Highbush blueberry	Spicebush
Inkberry	Summersweet
Live oak	Tamarack
	Willow

Know Your Zone

The United States Department of Agriculture's cold-hardiness zones, numbered from 1 to 11, with subcategories *a* and *b* within each zone, indicate the average winter low temperatures in each zone. This is crucial information, but it also can be misleading. It is crucial, because if you live in zone 5 and buy plants listed as hardy to zone 8, they will die when it gets too cold.

The lower the zone number, the colder the expected winter lows. Plants that won't survive the lowest expected average temperatures are a waste of money. But the zone numbers can be misleading because we don't have many average winters.

MORE

DIRT CHEAP

When buying trees, shrubs, or perennials, don't waste your money on plants that are not cold hardy to your area. In fact, opt for those that can withstand the next coldest zone. That way when a colder-than-average winter occurs, your carefully spent plant dollars will not be wasted.

USDA Cold-Hardiness Zones

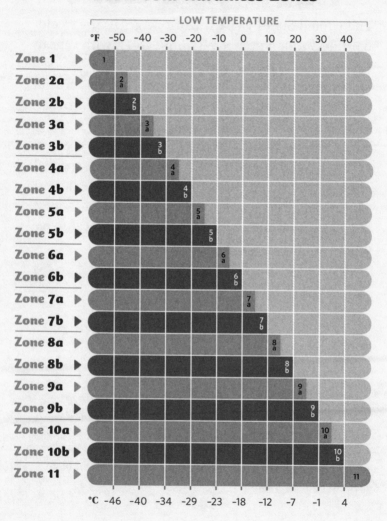

LOW TEMPERATURE

	°F	-50	-40	-30	-20	-10	0	10	20	30	40
Zone 1 ▶	1										
Zone 2a ▶		2a									
Zone 2b ▶		2b									
Zone 3a ▶			3a								
Zone 3b ▶			3b								
Zone 4a ▶				4a							
Zone 4b ▶				4b							
Zone 5a ▶					5a						
Zone 5b ▶					5b						
Zone 6a ▶						6a					
Zone 6b ▶						6b					
Zone 7a ▶							7a				
Zone 7b ▶							7b				
Zone 8a ▶								8a			
Zone 8b ▶								8b			
Zone 9a ▶									9a		
Zone 9b ▶									9b		
Zone 10a ▶										10a	
Zone 10b ▶										10b	
Zone 11 ▶											11
°C		-46	-40	-34	-29	-23	-18	-12	-7	-1	4

Pollution Solutions

Those who garden in areas beset by smog know it's even more devastating to plants than to people. Losses of crops, ornamentals, turf grass, and trees in the United States are estimated at over a billion dollars per year. The worst damage occurs during air inversions — when warmer air above traps cooler, thicker, more toxic air closer to ground level.

Cumulative damage, such as leaf or needle burning on trees, is most evident in the late summer or fall, after a growing season spent absorbing poisons. Plants weakened by air pollution are more susceptible to pests, diseases, drought, and nutrient deficiencies.

Despite all this, Los Angeles has some of the lushest gardens you'll ever see. What's the secret? It lies in selecting plants that can tolerate less-than-ideal growing conditions.

MORE

Pollution-Resistant Plants

Note: Some plants may be resistant to some pollutants but susceptible to others. Generally, plants with smaller leaves and flowers (petunias are a good example) tolerate pollution better than larger leaved/flowered varieties. Interestingly, white petunias don't do as well in high pollution areas as do blue, red, or purple.

Annual Vegetables and Ornamentals

Coleus
Cosmos
Four-o'clock
Madagascar periwinkle
Marigold
Moonflower
Pansy
Spiderflower
Sultana
Sunflower

Perennial Vegetables and Ornamentals

Alfalfa
Asparagus
Bergenia
Clematis
Climbing hydrangea
Columbine
Daylily
Grapes (some)
Hosta
Iris
Monarda
  (Beauty of Cobham)
Peppermint
Rudbeckia
Sedum
Trumpet vine
Virginia creeper

Trees/Shrubs

Apricot
Austrian pine
Berberis
  (Sunjoy Gold Beret)
Birches
Bradford pear
Flowering cherry
Flowering plum
Gingko
Magnolia sieboldii
Maple
Oak
Poplar
Weigela
  (Pink Delight)
Willow

Pollution-Susceptible Plants

Annual Vegetables and Ornamentals

Barley	Eggplant	Onion	Squash
Bean, green	Geranium	Petunia	Sultana
Bean, white	Lettuce	Potato	Sweet corn
Beet	Marigold	Pumpkin	Swiss chard
Buckwheat	Morning glory	Radish	Tomato
China aster	Muskmelon	Rutabaga	Wax begonia
Corn	Oats	Spinach	Zinnia
Cucumber			

Perennial Vegetables and Ornamentals

Alfalfa	Grape	Rhubarb	Strawberry
Aster	Raspberry	Rose	Tulip
Gladiolus			

Trees/Shrubs

Apple	Citrus	Peach	Weeping willow
Apricot	Forsythia	Plum	White ash
Aspen	Maple, silver and sugar	Poplar, hybrid	White oak
Blueberry		Prune	

The NASA Clean Air Study identified plants that serve as cheap indoor air filters by removing harmful chemicals. Bamboo palm, Boston fern, chrysanthemum, dracaenas, English ivy, golden pothos, philodendrons, rubber plants, and spider plant, among others, were found to eliminate significant amounts of benzene, formaldehyde, and trichloroethylene. Flowering houseplants, gerbera daisy, and chrysanthemum cleansed the air of benzene, while peace lily and chrysanthemum reduced trichloroethylene levels.

Consider Containers

What? Your garden site doesn't abide by *any* of the recommendations for a perfect site? Even if you are at the bottom of the north slope of a parking lot, you can still grow plants. The solution is to plant in containers. The key is using the right planting medium.

Almost any container will accommodate some type of plant. The biggest mistake gardeners make with containers is shoveling garden soil into them — it compacts when used in containers. Compacted soil squeezes out oxygen, dries out easily, and is difficult to wet again thoroughly. All this results in unhealthy plants. Even though dirt from your yard is free, using it alone in containers will cost you.

DIRT CHEAP

You can mix your own growing medium for less money than you can buy it. If you incorporate garden soil in your mix, you'll save even more.

Use only a rich, loamy soil and sift out any clods, stones, sticks, or other foreign matter. Garden soil teems with tiny life forms, from visible bugs to invisible ones. Healthy transplants and established plants can tolerate raw soil in the mix. If you are starting seeds, however, use a germination mix.

Container growing is easy and can be cheap. The most important investment is not the container but the growing medium. Here's a standard formula for mixing planting medium:

- ▶ 1 part soil
- ▶ 1 part peat moss
- ▶ 1 part perlite, vermiculite, or sharp, clean sand
- ▶ 1 part compost (optional)

Find a container large enough to suit your needs and stir in the above ingredients until thoroughly mixed.

You can customize mixes for the type of plants you are growing. For plants requiring free drainage, such as cacti or succulents, add an extra part of sand or perlite. For those with specific nutritional requirements, mix in fertilizer accordingly.

Choosing Containers

There are many options for planting containers, but before you choose one, here are a few things to consider.

▶ **Will you be raising food or ornamentals in it?** Never grow food crops in containers that have previously contained any substance that is toxic, unknown, or questionable. Plant roots transport many toxins; they could end up on your dinner table.

▶ **Does the container have sufficient drainage?** Poor drainage kills off plants. A larger container requires more and larger holes.

▶ **What is the container made of?** Metal containers get very hot in direct sun and transmit the heat to tender plant roots. Black plastic pots absorb more heat than light-colored ones, but keep in mind that many plants, such as poinsettias, must have their roots in a dark environment.

Wood containers may harbor fungi, and stone or brick containers absorb heat, then release it slowly. Terra cotta or clay pots are decorative, but they absorb water away from plant roots; peat pots also absorb water from roots, so be sure to keep plants evenly watered.

DIRT CHEAP

Lovely, decorative containers abound in trendy garden centers, and they can set you back a few bucks if you must have them. But creativity and an eye for unusual items are free. Create your own plant containers from found and recycled objects, large and small.

Salvage an old pair of cowboy boots, and fill them with lobelia or ivy geraniums. An old wheelbarrow makes a purposeful planter, deep enough for carrots, large enough for broccoli, and decorative enough for a variety of flowers and trailing vines.

Wooden crates, dented metal buckets, plastic-lined wicker baskets, hollowed-out logs, old watering cans, antique milk cans, discarded lunch boxes, junked claw-foot bathtubs, unseaworthy rowboats or canoes, and countless other finds make fun, functional, frugal planters. See what you can find.

Soil Toil

Thou shalt not skimp on soil preparation! The more you put into your soil, the more you will get out of it. What, you may ask, is the big deal? Dirt is still dirt, right? The truth is your soil health predicts the health of your entire garden. Rich, nutritious soil sustains healthy plants that are more productive and give you the best possible return for your gardening investment. As you garden, they also cost little or nothing in pesticides, fertilizers, and replacement.

DIRT CHEAP

Incorporating humus into your garden can be as cheap or expensive as you make it. Not surprisingly, the cheaper ways are more work than the expensive ones. The ideal way to incorporate humus is to make your own by composting (see pages 148–154 for information about compost piles). Barnyard manures also provide plenty of partially processed organic matter.

Of course, garden centers make things easy by offering bags of dried organic matter in the form of peat moss, processed compost, and cow manure. The advantage of products containing fertilizers is they also contain soil nutrients, usually including necessary nitrogen. So while it is less expensive to compost your own, the good news about buying bags of humus is that your money will be well spent.

Cultivate a Sense of Humus

Soil provides physical support for the plants and a reservoir for nutrients, water, and oxygen. Some soils do the second part better than others. Sandy soils drain quickly, providing plenty of oxygen, but they also lose water and dissolve nutrients too quickly. Clay holds minerals and moisture well but drains poorly. The magic ingredient for improving either type of soil, or any type in between, is humus.

Humus is organic matter that has gone through a degrading experience. Organic matter is the remains of previously living things, such as plants, microorganisms, bugs, and us. When added to sandy soils, humus improves water retention by attracting water molecules. When added to clay, humus improves drainage by breaking up the clay particles that naturally cling together. Humus also provides fuel for millions of microorganisms that reside in the soil. As they break it down, the microorganisms release elements necessary for plant growth.

High levels of humus are a sign of well-managed soil. It is best to add small amounts of humus each year and build it up, rather than dump it all on in one application. This is important because in the process of decaying organic matter, microorganisms tie up precious soil nitrogen, which must be replenished. A good rule of thumb is to add not more than 4 inches of organic matter each year to any garden area.

GREEN THUMB

What Plants Need to Eat

The major nutrients needed by plants are those listed on plant-food labels as N (nitrogen), P (phosphorus), and K (potassium, available as potash or K_2O). Think of nitrogen as food for green, leafy parts of plants; phosphorus for roots and fruits; and potassium for general well-being, including resistance to cold and disease.

Sometimes labels include a fourth value for sulfur, a secondary, but still necessary, element. Sulfur (usable by plants only in the form of sulfate or SO_4), is an important part of amino acids (and therefore plant proteins), chlorophyll, some vitamins and hormones, carbohydrate metabolism, root growth, and overall plant vitality and hardiness.

Dirt Cheap

Many soils are naturally high or low in some of the necessary elements, but nitrogen is the most water soluble and therefore the most likely to leach away (and into groundwater supplies). Adding more nitrogen than plants can take up is a waste of money, however, so don't go overboard.

The elements plants use less of are called secondary elements. They are no less critical to healthy growth than the major elements; plants just require smaller doses of them. In addition to sulfur, they are calcium (Ca) and magnesium (Mg). Don't waste money by adding these to your soil on a yearly basis because plants take them in slowly, and they don't leach away. A single application usually lasts several years.

Trace or micronutrients are those of which plants require only small amounts. They include boron (B), manganese (Mn), copper (Cu), zinc (Zn), iron (Fe), molybdenum (Mo), and chlorine (Cl). Short of a soil test, the best way to tell if you need to add any of these is by plant response.

The most important thing to remember in applying nitrogen fertilizers is that the plants will show the effects most dramatically in three to four weeks, so time your applications accordingly. Adding excess nitrogen in the summer — especially to food crops that must bear fruit, such as tomatoes, peppers, squash, and melons — results in all green and little to no fruit. Adding nitrogen to woody plants after midsummer can cause them to put out new green growth when they should be preparing for dormancy, resulting in winter damage or dieback.

GREEN THUMB

Cheap Soil Amendments

Let's consider some low-cost soil amendments, where you can get them, and how they will help your garden.

▶ **Mushroom compost** is excellent, if you happen to live near a commercial grower. This used compost is still rich in nutrients and organic matter; a few little mushrooms may pop up, but since you know they are edible, eat up.

▶ **Sewage sludge** is treated using two methods, anaerobic digestion and air activation. Digested sludge is much lower quality as a fertilizer than the activated type, but activated sludge is usually much more expensive. Either type of heat-treated sludge is safe to use around your yard and garden. Inquire at your local treatment plant.

▶ **Green vegetation** spaded into the soil adds precious organic matter, nutrients, and moisture. Use green leaves, weeds, grass clippings, and cover crops such as clovers, buckwheat, rye, and oats. Legumes, such as clover, vetch, and alfalfa, take nitrogen from the air and convert it into a usable form for plants.

▶ **Coffee grounds** from espresso bars or coffee brewers are a good source of nitrogen. Ask the brewer to empty coffee grounds into a container for you to pick up once a week. The grounds are fairly acidic and useful in lowering pH levels when heavily applied.

▶ **Sawdust** is a good form of organic matter for your garden. Don't add more than 2 inches each year, because for each ton of sawdust, a garden burns about 3½ pounds of pure nitrogen. Offset this loss by adding 17 pounds of ammonium sulfate, 11 pounds of ammonium nitrate, or 8 pounds of urea. Avoid cedar sawdust; it's toxic to some seedlings. Alderwood dust decomposes more quickly than others, such as fir or hemlock.

▶ **Animal manures** are a good amendment, but you should never use cat, dog, or swine (or, for heaven's sake, human) manure in your garden because they may harbor parasites and disease organisms that can be harmful to your health. Racetracks, livestock breeding farms, dairy farms, rabbit runs, poultry farms, and zoos often are overjoyed to have someone actually volunteer to haul the manure away!

Fresh manure is not recommended for use in the garden, as it contains disease-causing bacteria, as well as high concentrations of salts that can burn plant roots. Also, some people find the aroma objectionable. Compost it or allow it to age six months to a year before applying to the garden, or spread it over the soil in the fall so it has time to mellow before planting season.

GREEN THUMB

pH for Gardeners

Just as some plants naturally prefer sun or shade, dampness or dryness, some are more than a little finicky about soil pH. Technically, pH is defined as the negative logarithm of hydrogen ion concentration. Put more simply, it is a measure of acidity or alkalinity. It's important to know how it affects plants.

Generally, soils in places with wet climates tend to be acidic and those in dry areas tend to be alkaline. Native plants adapt to their soils, so plants do exist to suit almost any type of soil. However, most garden plants prefer soils with a pH between 6.0 and 7.0. This may not sound like much of a difference, but it is.

The pH scale runs from 0 to 14, with 0 being the most acidic and 14 the most alkaline (or basic), and 7 neutral. Each number represents a 10-fold difference, so soil that has a pH of 6 is 10 times more acidic than soil with a pH of 7. To put this into perspective, battery acid has a pH of about 1, and lemon juice's pH is about 2. Which would you rather get on your skin?

DIRT CHEAP

Soil pH can be amended — even somewhat reliably over time — but it's far cheaper and easier to choose plants that prefer your yard the way it is.

Keep an Eye on pH Levels

Soil pH can change as much as a full point during the growing season. Just as temperature and moisture vary over the months, so too does the soil pH. Acidity is a function of hydrogen ions in solution; i.e., dissolved in water. Let the soil dry out, and the pH value is skewed because there is no solution.

So while there's not much you can do to control the temperature, monitoring it and soil moisture will go a long ways toward maintaining your soil pH, its nutrient levels, and your plants' health.

Tomatoes Tell All

In addition to the joys of eating them, tomato plants are useful for their diagnostic skills. They are sensitive to soil abnormalities and show distinct symptoms in response to soil deficiencies. For instance, the youngest leaves of tomatoes grown in iron-deficient soils turn yellow between the veins, with the base of the leaflets showing the most discoloration.

In calcium-poor soils the youngest leaves turn purplish brown, and eventually the fruit rots at the blossom end. Purple veins indicate a phosphorus deficiency (often caused by too-cold growing conditions).

Taking (Soil) Tests

If your plants are not performing well or you have just built a new home on subsoil battered by heavy machinery, testing your soil makes sense. If you wish to grow acid-loving plants, such as blueberries, get an inexpensive pH meter, and test routinely. You have several options.

▶ **The Garden Center Variety.** This type of test lets you play with test tubes, litmus paper, or electronic probes. The least expensive give an accurate reading of pH, while higher-priced models also break down nutrient levels. There are full kits available that measure everything but man-made contaminants, as well as various gadgets that measure moisture, temperature, and light. With so many tests available, it's easy to get carried away, so buy only the kit(s) that tests for what you need to know.

▶ **The Professional Assessment.** Professional labs, through an agricultural extension service or a private company, perform more thorough tests. You send in a sample of dirt, and the lab sends back a long list of specific data and a bill that can run anywhere from a few dollars for a simple pH test to around $50.

The Do-It-Yourself Option

The cheapest soil test is to look around at the native plants; i.e., weeds (see list on next page). Weed reading is a time-tested skill. With practice, it can tell you more about your soil and growing conditions than all the litmus paper and lab fees in the world. Here are some guidelines:

▶ **Look for perennials.** They are stronger indicators of overall long-term conditions than annuals.

▶ **Look for groups of plants with similar preferences.** Plant communities flourish where conditions are consistent.

▶ **Defer to the finicky.** The more specific a plant's requirements, the more it reveals about the conditions under which it is found.

▶ **Factor in growth habit.** The condition of weeds says as much as their presence. A great example: Flourishing leguminous weeds, such as clover or vetch, along with puny, pale, nonleguminous weeds, such as knapweed or plantain, indicate soil that is low in nitrogen.

▶ **Give all forces their due.** Plants growing in areas you suspect to be damp, acidic, and shady may be there in response to all or just one of those factors.

▶ **Notice what's missing.** The absence of certain plants says as much as the presence of others.

Native Plants as Soil Indicators

Grow in Acid Soil

Bracken

Cinquefoil

Clover

Coltsfoot

Dandelion

Dock

English daisy

Horsetail

Knapweed

Mullein

Nettle

Ox-eye daisy

Pansy, wild

Parsnip, wild

Plantain

Red cedar

Sorrel

Stinking mayweed (or stinking chamomile)

Strawberry, wild

Grow in Alkaline Soils

Bladder campion

Carrot, wild

Chickweed

Chicory

Goosefoot

Henbane, black

Mustard

Nodding thistle

Queen Anne's lace

Spotted spurge

Grow in Poor Soil

Bracken (P, K)

Medic, black (N)

Mugwort

Mullein

Ox-eye daisy

Radish, wild

Rape (N)

Vetch (N)

Wormwood

Yarrow (K)

Grow in Dry Soil

Agrimony

Cinquefoil, silvery

Clover, white sweet

Russian thistle

Speedwell

St. John's wort

Grow in Wet Soil

Bellflower, creeping

Coltsfoot

Dock

Foxtail

Goldenrod

Hellebore, false

Hemlock

Joe-Pye weed

Meadowsweet

Morning glory

Moss

Ox-eye daisy

Ragwort, tansy

Rushes

Sedges

Skunk cabbage

Sorrel

Water hemlock

KEY: P = Low phosphorus, N = Low nitrogen, K = Low potassium

Signs of Stress

Overall soil infertility will result in small, unthrifty-looking plants that may fail to flower, fruit, or even survive. If your soil lacks any given nutrient that affects your plants, they will tell you. For example, slow, stunted growth and yellowing foliage of older leaves signify a lack of nitrogen.

Phosphorus deficiencies are harder to spot but generally result in stunted early growth. Lack of potassium is common to light or poor soils and shows up in fruit crops as "burning" and curling of leaf tips and edges, yellowing of leaf veins, and a lack of frost and disease resistance.

Help! My Soil Flunked the Test!

What can be done if testing reveals that your soil is too high or low in pH or lacking in a particular nutrient? The first rule of penny-pinching gardeners is to work with what you have. Plant plants that like your garden soil just the way it is. See the following lists for suggestions.

DIRT CHEAP

Be sure soil is dry before testing. Moisture can cause false results. Perform commercial or lab soil tests in the late fall or early spring so that any amendments you make have time to take effect before planting season.

Plants That Tolerate Acid Soil

Perennials & Flowers

Aster*
Barrenwort
Bearberry
Begonia, wax
Bleeding heart
Butterfly weed
Calla lily
Coralbells
Cosmos
Foxglove

Gentian
Hardy ferns, most varieties
Heath*
Heather*
Lady slipper
Lily of the Valley
Lupine
Marigold
Pansy
Phlox

Primrose
Snapdragon
Trillium*
Tulip
Virginia
  bluebell
Winterberry
Wintergreen
Woodland
  phlox
Zinnia

Food Crops

Beans
Blackberry
Blueberry*
Brussels sprout
Carrot
Cauliflower
Collard
Cucumber
Eggplant
Garlic

Grapes
Kale
Mustard
Parsley
Peas
Pepper
Potato
Pumpkin
Radish
Raspberry

Rhubarb
Spinach
Squash
Strawberry
Sweet corn
Sweet potato
Tomato
Turnip
Watermelon

Trees

Alder
Apple
Apricot
Birch
Buckeye
Fir
Hemlock

Horse chestnut
Larch (tamarack)*
Magnolia
Mountain ash
Nectarine
Oak
Pagoda dogwood

Peach
Pear
Pine
Pin oak
Spruce
Yew, upright

Shrubs

Azalea

Bog rosemary

Camelia*

Dogwood*

Dwarf hemlock

Dwarf spruce

False cypress

Hydrangea, blue*

Juniper

Mountain laurel

Mugo pine

Rhododendron

Rose

Serviceberry

Sweetbush

Winterberry

Yew

Prefers moderately acid to highly acid soil

Plants That Tolerate Alkaline Soil

Flowers & Ornamentals

Ageratum

Bergenia*

Carnation

Clematis

Corydalis*

Cosmos

Gypsophila*

Marigold

Pachysandra

Peony*

Pincushion flower

Snapdragon

Sweet alyssum

Trumpet vine

Wisteria

Yarrow, fernleaf*

Vegetables

Asparagus*

Beet*

Broccoli*

Cabbage*

Carrot*

Cauliflower*

Celery*

Cress

Leek

Lettuce*

Muskmelon

Okra

Onion

Parsley*

Spinach

Trees & Shrubs

Almond

Arrowwood viburnum

Box elder

Boxwood*

Cherry

Cotoneaster*

Euonymus*

Forsythia*

Hackberry

Horse chestnut

Lilac*

Locust

Mock orange*

Plum

Potentilla*

Rugosa rose*

Sargent crabapple

Prefers moderately alkaline to highly alkaline soil

Adding Amendments

If you have a yen for plants with particular require-ments that your garden doesn't naturally supply, then soil amendments are likely in order. Gardeners com-monly alter pH with lime, which reduces acidity, and ammonium nitrate and sulfur, which raise acidity. (Note: In soils with lots of free lime, lowering the pH through chemical enhancements is an expensive and all-too-often disappointing process.)

Other soil additives also affect pH balance. One of the best ways to lower pH is to work in peat or sphag-num peat, as this not only helps to acidify soil but also incorporates plenty of beneficial organic matter. Manures, sludge, coffee grounds, sulfur, and high-nitrogen fertilizers also raise acidity.

Soil amendments must be mixed in well, and soil must be kept moist (to provide a solution) and aerated (bacteria need oxygen to do their job) for pH levels to adjust. Letting the soil dry out or compact after add-ing amendments simply wastes your time and money. Warm temperatures also help, as bacteria thrive in the warmth.

A Cheap Secret Weapon?

Many gardeners believe that including a tablespoon (14.3 g) of Epsom salts (magnesium sulfate) in the planting hole of tomato and pepper transplants boosts growth, as does a foliar spray of one tablespoon of dissolved salts to a gallon (3.8 L) of water. It's also considered a handy amendment in potted indoor plants for dissolving accumulated salts from plant roots and thereby allowing them to take up other nutrients.

Although magnesium sulfate has been proven to boost the production and health of intensively gardened crops on *magnesium-poor* soil, the raft of other claims as to the benefits of this common household item says more about our longing for cheap, simple fixes than our powers of observation. Studies show that overdosing with magnesium sulfate can burn young leaves, and even though it is very soluble and quickly runs off through soil, it doesn't disappear. It winds up somewhere.

So the secret weapon is to keep your sense of skepticism, even though it may mean giving up a cheap garden tip. With Mother Nature there are no wonder drugs or easy fixes. Always consider the consequences, both good and bad.

MORE

Amendments at a Glance

If a professional soil test indicates any of the following conditions, the correct amendment should fix the problem.

Problem	Solution
pH too high	Add sulfur or other acidifying agents
pH too low	Add lime
Nitrogen deficient	Add nitrogen-rich fertilizer
Nitrogen too high	Stop fertilizing! Plant high-nitrogen feeders such as corn to metabolize excess nitrogen or water heavily to leach it out.
Phosphorus deficient	Add superphosphate, bone meal, rock phosphate or colloidal phosphate, or other phosphorous-rich amendments.
Phosphorus too high	Use only low-phosphorus fertilizer and plant heavy phosphorus feeders, such as root crops, to metabolize excess phosphorus.
Potassium deficient	Add wood ashes or potash. (Note: Wood ashes are alkaline and shouldn't be used around acid-loving plants.)
Potassium too high	Balance with a nitrogen/phosphorus–rich fertilizer, but avoid potassium-rich fertilizers.

Calcium deficiency	Most common in sandy or acid soil. Add gypsum, Epsom salts or, if soil is too acid, dolomitic limestone.
Too much calcium (calcium carbonate)	Treat as for alkaline soil. Add soil amendments to acidify (lower pH).
Magnesium deficiency	Add dolomitic lime or Epsom salts (hydrated magnesium sulfate).
Too much magnesium	Add calcium.
Sulfur deficiency	Add ammonium sulfate, gypsum, or elemental sulfur.
Too much sulfur	Generally not a problem.
Light soil/drains too fast	Work in organic matter, such as peat moss, to improve water retention.
Heavy soil/drains too slowly	Work in organic matter, such as peat moss, to break up compact soil and improve drainage.

DIRT CHEAP

Young plants are very sensitive to pH levels, and it takes time for the process to work, so it's best to add amendments the season *before* you plant to give the additive time to change the acid balance. Apply lime at least 30 days prior to using fertilizers; they bind each other up when applied together, essentially wasting the money spent on both products.

Water, Water (Not) Everywhere

How you deliver water to your plants will have a major impact on your watering costs. If you are on a community water supply, you can cut your monthly bill significantly with wily watering. If you water from a well, you will save on the cost of running a pump. Either way you will conserve water.

In the past we merely turned on the sprinkler and walked away; today water conservation is a top priority. Water bills are not the only reason — drought and heavy demand call for careful management of this most precious resource.

GREEN THUMB

Using a lawn sprinkler or an overhead watering system on hot, windy days wastes a lot of water. The idea of watering is to deliver an adequate amount of water to the roots — no more, no less, and nowhere else. Choose a sprinkler that targets the roots or better yet, install a system of soaker hoses.

Several factors determine how much water you need to apply and the best method of application:

▶ **Amount of rainfall.** No matter what plants you are watering in what type of soil, the amount of watering necessarily depends on how much nature already supplies.

▶ **Type of soil.** Remember that sandy soils drain quickly and that clay holds moisture. These are functions of how the water moves through the soil, which affects its availability to plant roots.

▶ **Type of plants.** Some plants need much more water than others. New plants, from seeded lawns to bedding transplants and burlap-balled shrubs, require lots of frequent watering to establish their roots. Established native plants need very little rainfall supplementation; they have naturally adapted to the area.

DIRT CHEAP

Hand watering wastes as much time as it does water. Unless you stand there for a few hours with a water wand, you cannot wet the soil deeply enough to do a worthwhile job.

How Much Water?

While there is no single answer to the question of how much water is just right, most plants should be watered deeply and infrequently. The most efficient and cost-effective way to water is to soak the entire root zone with water and let the soil become almost dry before the next watering.

The amount of dryness depends on the plant. Let the top 2 or 3 inches dry out for most established plants, but keep new or tiny plants moist to the top inch or so of soil.

▶ **Lawns:** Water to a depth of at least 6 inches as soon as grass fails to spring up after walking on it. Frequent, shallow waterings lead to shallow roots, which are far more susceptible to heat or drought. Renting an aerator every other year or so will help to reduce thatch buildup and combat compaction.

▶ **Bedding plants and perennials:** Water established plants 6 to 12 inches deep every 4 to 10 days, but don't wait for plants to wilt before the next watering. Wilting slows growth and reduces crop yields. Soaker hoses or drip irrigation can save up to 60 percent of the water used by a sprinkler. Place mulch over the hose to prevent evaporation.

▶ **Trees, shrubs, and landscape plants:** Water throughout the dripline (the area around the circumference) of plants for the most efficient intake of water. This is where the newest, most active root growth is found. Soaker hoses allow you to deliver water to individual plants and are great for shrubs that are susceptible to moisture-loving disease organisms.

▶ **Vegetables and other food crops:** These are big exception to the "let the soil dry out" rule, as nearly constant moisture ensures quick, even growth, tenderness, and peak flavor. Gardening in raised beds with soaker hoses or drip lines is the ideal way to keep crop soils evenly moist. Container watering works great for large, thirsty, individual plants such as tomatoes and peppers, provided the containers are kept refilled.

GREEN THUMB

To make sure you are delivering enough water to where it is needed, use a soil probe or shovel before you water to determine the extent of dryness. Repeat the process after watering to see how deeply the water has penetrated into the soil.

Break up the surface of unmulched soil every week or so to increase water absorption. Otherwise, the soil will form a crust at the surface, creating a barrier against water penetration.

Ways to Stop Water Loss

In a perfect world every drop of water you put on your plants would run straight to the roots and would be used immediately by the plant. But we have to deal with water loss. Knowing how to reduce it saves water and money.

▶ **Add humus.** Humus is a water magnet. By incorporating lots of humus into the soil, you will lessen the amount of water that percolates through the soil and out of reach.

▶ **Reduce evaporation.** Thanks to capillary action through the soil, which draws water up from below, evaporation can deplete water from deep in the ground. Keeping the soil

DIRT CHEAP

If water is scarce or expensive in your area, the frugal thing to do is choose plants that require less water in the first place. Group together plants that need heavier watering so you can concentrate the water in just a few locations. If your yard has a naturally moist microclimate, put the water hogs there. It's easier to keep a low pocket moist than a raised berm. Position sprinklers to avoid watering sidewalks, streets, decks, and other structures that won't grow.

surface covered with mulch (see pages 184–187) protects against this. Another line of defense against evaporation is to get less of the soil surface wet in the first place. This means replacing a sprinkler with a drip system, soaker hose, or individual water containers for landscape or large vegetable plants.

▶ **Counter transpiration.** On a hot summer day, one large shade tree can transpire several *hundred* gallons of water through its leaves. Misting plants on hot, dry days helps limit the amount transpired and reduces plant stress.

▶ **Time yourself.** Water early in the morning or at night and never water during hot, windy weather.

Mounding the soil around the dripline of a shrub helps retain water.

DIRT CHEAP

A cheap version of drip irrigation is container watering. Bury containers, such as a plastic gallon (3.8 L) milk jug with two or three small holes punched in the bottom (use a large nail or make slits with a knife), next to or in between individual plants. Leave the caps off and keep the containers filled with water, allowing it to seep directly into plant root zones. Tailor the size of the container to the size of the plant.

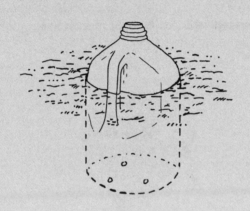

Climb on the Rain Barrel

Most of us have more water than we know what to do with. Even in arid regions there are occasional deluges of rain. Rain barrels are not a new idea, but they are still a useful one. Position clean, empty barrels beneath downspouts or up on blocks around the garden. A simple mesh screen fitted over the top will keep out debris and mosquitoes.

Barrels, positioned a few inches above the ground, can incorporate spigots and drip tubing for a cheap, gravity-flow irrigation system. A barrel positioned high above the ground creates strong water pressure, and far-flowing water. This time-honored method is excellent for flower or vegetable gardens.

You can set up a rain barrel equipped with spigot and drip tubing to make your own cheap gravity-flow irrigation system.

Pennywise Plants

It is impossible to overemphasize the importance of choosing plants carefully. Some plants just give you more for the money. While chapter 4 goes into details about specific recommended plants and varieties, I'd like to share some basic truths here.

One is that the most expensive plants are not necessarily the best. They may be rare, newly developed, or the result of years of research and plant breeding, but none of that ensures they are best for your garden.

Is Bigger Better?

There are many things to consider before spending your hard-earned dollars at the nursery. With landscaping especially, the size of the plants you buy determines your immediate results. But it is their size at maturity that determines how your yard will *eventually* look.

Younger plants are cheaper but take longer to fulfill your dreams of a perfect yard, unless they grow fast. With trees, smaller plants actually catch up with more mature ones in a few years and then grow faster and better.

The downside to quick-growing plants is that they often have a short life span. The pennywise answer is to use "fast growers" to give you something to show for your money right away, combined with "long livers" to sustain your investment.

Fast-Growing Plants

Acacia (T)
Blackeyed susan vine (V)
Bugleweed (G)
Butterfly bush (S)
Carpathian walnut (T)
Cistus (S)
Eucalyptus (T)
Flowering plum (T)
Fuchsia (S)
Hazelnut (T)
Hibiscus (S)

Hydrangea (S)
Lantana (S, V)
Maple (T)
Ornamental grasses (G)
Pine (T)
Poplar (T)
Quaking aspen (T)
Rose (S, V)
Sweet pea (V)
Willow (T)

Long-Lived Plants

Daylily* (P)
Flowering quince (S)
Forsythia (S)
Ginkgo (T)
Grape (V)
Hawthorn (S, T)

Lilac (S, T)
Maple (T)
Rhubarb (P)
Rose (old garden, ramblers) (S, V)
Wisteria (V)

Clumps, not necessarily the original plants, last indefinitely.
KEY: (G) Ground Cover; (P) Perennial; (S) Shrub; (T) Tree; (V)Vine

DIRT CHEAP

A dollar spent on a six-pack of petunias may seem like a bargain compared to three dollars for a single candytuft, until you multiply the cost over several years. Invest in longer-living plants and perennials that will come back year after year.

Longer Life Stretches Your Dollar

The longer a plant lives, the more you will get for your money. Food plants yield more crops over a longer period of time. Flowers, whether for cutting or bedding, bloom longer. Several factors limit longevity, however, not the least of which is genetics.

Like us, plants have a somewhat predetermined life span. The entire life cycle of annuals lasts a single season. Perennials come back every year. Though annuals are cheaper than perennials, you must replace them every year. The exceptions here are open-pollinated annuals that reseed, such as sweet alyssum, Johnny jump-ups, and California poppies. They essentially replant themselves every year for free, saving you both work and money (see page 89). Note that some hybrids can produce seed, but they will not grow true to the original variety.

TOOLS VERSUS TOYS

Ancient ruins reveal crude gardening instruments in the form of sticks with metal blades attached. Humans used clay urns to carry water. That was about it; there were no rototillers or riding lawn mowers. Yet somehow the human race evolved from hunter-gatherers to farmers.

If a few crude tools were enough to transform humanity, they are enough to get you by in the garden. Efficient, cost-effective gardening requires some tools, but not all gadgets are what they're cracked up to be. Knowing which tools are appropriate for which jobs will help you tell the tools from the toys.

Whether you opt for more sophisticated, expensive hardware depends on your priorities. If you really want to save money in the garden, only buy a tool if it does the job better than what you are using. Also, consider versatility when buying tools. The more one tool can do for you, the fewer tools you need.

People-Powered Tools

These are the fundamental tools necessary for gardening. They do not contribute to air or noise pollution, they cost virtually nothing to operate, and they require little cleaning and maintenance. Yet with a little people power, these tools perform any task in the garden.

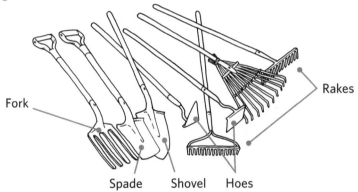

Fork

Rakes

Spade Shovel Hoes

DIRT CHEAP

Buy the best-quality tools you can afford, and take appropriate care of them. Cheap tools will cost you, in either repairs or replacement costs. Well-made tools last longer and require fewer repairs. Those necessary repairs are always cheaper than buying new tools.

Determining the Essentials

So how do you separate the tools from the toys? The answer depends on your gardening situation, your physical ability, and your pocketbook. Personally, I get by with the basics:

- A long-handled, rounded-point shovel

- A short-handled, square-point spade

- A short-handled spading fork

- A paddle hoe

- A couple of trowels and a handheld claw

- A large two-wheeled wheelbarrow

- My old trusty Swiss-made bypass pruners

- Several hoses, sprinklers, soaker hoses

- Good gloves and a big, floppy hat

Your basics may be more or less than mine, but a good rule is if you don't use it, lose it. Trade it for something you will use — or perhaps for more plants!

Cultivating Tools

Cultivating tools — forks, hoes, spades, rakes, trowels, claws, and rotary-wheeled, toothed cultivators — break up and move soil. They have a metal head and a wooden, metal, or plastic handle. Look for carbon steel or stainless steel heads. If kept clean and dry between uses, carbon steel should not rust.

Stainless steel is more expensive but is rustproof and makes work easier, as soil easily falls away from it. Coatings on blades can wear off over time, making coated blades a questionable expenditure.

Wooden handles, such as those made of hickory, are generally strong; buff to a warm, smooth glow through time and work; and, unlike metal or plastic, can be replaced if broken. Buy a handle that is of a comfortable length and angle for you to use.

Forks

Forks (also called spading forks) are versatile tools that allow you to loosen and cultivate soil, move bulky materials such as weed piles, work compost and manure piles, and lift root crops. Most forks have four sturdy metal prongs attached to a wooden or metal shaft.

The best-quality forks are those with the prongs and neck forged from a single piece of metal. Avoid forks that are pieced together or welded. Short-handled handheld forks lift up plants and work well for knee-level weeding.

Hoes

Hoes cultivate, weed, and form seed rows. They have long or short handles with a blade attached. There are several types of hoes with specific uses.

▶ **Paddle hoes** chop weeds and dirt.

▶ **Dutch hoes** and **scuffle**, **stirrup**, or **oscillating hoes** work well to remove small, surface weeds around plants and to cultivate just below the soil surface. Scuffle hoes are easy on the gardener, as the blade cuts both pushing and pulling.

▶ The **heart hoe**, named for its heart-shaped blade, was designed by a frustrated gardener to slice underneath sod. The groove at the top of the "heart" also snags and yanks up weeds.

▶ A **combination hoe** has prongs on one side for breaking up soil and a blade on the other for chopping or moving around soil.

▶ A **triangular-headed hoe** creates V-shaped furrows and digs weeds out of narrow spots.

▶ **Gooseneck hoes** have long, swanlike handles, engineered to allow you to work around plants and in tight places.

▶ **Handheld hoes** have short handles and small, narrow blades for cultivating between closely spaced plants.

Rakes

Rakes cultivate surface soil, create an even and level soil surface, and rake debris. Those with wider heads work the fastest, because they cover more ground each time you rake. **Lawn rakes,** compared to **cultivating rakes,** are lightweight and have flexible tines designed to move light debris such as leaves or mown grass. **Flathead rakes** break up dirt clods and catch small stones and debris on the toothed side. They're generally heavier and sturdier than welded **bowhead** types but because of the weight can be more tiring to use. Flip over either style to use the flat surface as a smoothing edge.

Spades and Shovels

Spades and shovels dig and turn soil and lift plants. Spades are made to chop into the dirt and loosen it, as when you're edging an area. Shovels have a curve at the neck to help dig in and lift and move dirt. Every gardener needs a **rounded-point shovel** to dig into soil, turn it over, and move it and to lift out or move plants around. A **square-pointed spade** comes in handy to move dirt, compost, or manure from one place to another.

Calling a Spade a Shovel

A transplanting spade is actually a shovel and is also called a drain spade shovel (that helps, right?). It has a long, narrow blade designed to dig up plants without disturbing its neighbors.

DIRT CHEAP

When buying digging implements, it's worth splurging on stainless steel as it takes a lot of strain out of digging and won't rust. Otherwise, for strength and longevity, opt for a carbon steel blade. Just don't waste your money on nonstick coatings. As soon as the coating wears off, so does your extra investment. Also, look for a blade with a flattened area at the top where you rest (or stomp!) your feet. It will save wear and tear on you and your garden clogs.

Trowels

Trowels are mini-shovels that are great for planting and digging small transplanting holes. They are especially handy for working in containers. Rubber handle grips make them easier on your hands, and ergonomically designed models ward off wrist injury. The blades are somewhat cupped, and can be wide or narrow.

Claw Weeders

Claw weeders target weeds, cultivate, and mix soil with a twist of the handle. The downside is they only work about a 6-inch-diameter area with each effort, but for people who have a difficult time reaching and pulling, they can be helpful. The prongs or teeth break up the soil but work well only after the soil has already been cultivated and only to a shallow depth.

Rotary Cultivators

Rotary cultivators have spinning teeth that work and aerate soil quickly with each pass. They do an admirable job of disturbing surface soil (to aid water absorption) and mixing in amendments but only work to a depth of 2 or 3 inches (depending on the model).

Where the Deals Are

Whether you are shopping for hand tools, power equipment, or garden décor, consider the following sources:

▶ Thrift shops

▶ Flea markets

▶ Yard sales

▶ Estate sales

▶ Pawnshops

▶ End-of-season sales at garden centers and hardware stores

▶ Want ads

▶ Internet sources such as Craigslist and Freecycle

Pruning Tools

Pruning tools cut woody growth. Pruning is necessary to keep many plants in their prime, to control plant growth and shape, and to facilitate blooming. Short- or long-handled pruners, saws, and knives are examples of handheld pruning tools.

Pruners

Pruners come in two types. **Bypass pruners** have two slicing blades that cleanly snip stems, twigs, or dead blossoms. They are the most versatile. **Anvil pruners** work by pushing a single blade into the stem as it is held against a flat pad. Unless kept *very* sharp, they crush stems. Buy pruners that give a clean, crisp cut; ragged edges leave plants open to infection. Coated grips are worth the expense; they are more comfortable to use than bare steel.

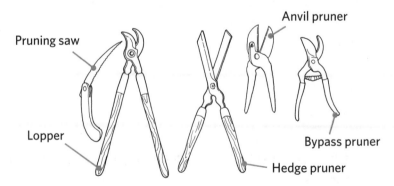

High-quality pruners with stainless or carbon steel blades are worth the investment. Their clean, crisp cuts help prevent plant infection.

Loppers

Loppers are long-handled pruners used to cut branches in hard-to-reach places. The leverage created by the long handles makes cutting small branches a snap, and the shears can handle limbs 2 inches thick or more.

Tree Pruners

Tree pruners cut high branches. They work on a lever system, and some models can extend your reach up to 15 feet. For most jobs, though, a ladder and loppers will suffice.

Saws

Saws prune heavy branches. Of the several types available, a **Grecian saw** is one of the most versatile. It has a curved handle and teeth designed to cut only as you pull toward yourself, making it easier to use in tight spaces. **Bow saws** work quickly but are unwieldy to use in close quarters.

DIRT CHEAP

Get the best-quality stainless or carbon steel blades you can afford, and be sure they can be resharpened. Though I winced at the initial purchase price, I've had the same pair of Swiss-made pruners for almost 30 years. Choose a pair with replaceable parts, and they will likely outlast you.

Making the Earth Move

Wheelbarrows and garden carts are invaluable tools for saving your back as you move heavy piles of dirt, rocks, and other debris around your garden. Wheelbarrows come in single-wheeled styles, double-wheeled types, collapsible models, and one that rolls on a ball instead of a tire, said to be suitable for use on mud, sand, or snow.

Sizes with a capacity of 6 to 8 cubic feet, able to carry up to 300 pounds, are most common, though the ball-wheeled model is rated for up to 750 pounds. Spring for the toughest, not necessarily the biggest, model you can afford. Contractors' wheelbarrows are reinforced and have sturdy wheels.

Double-wheeled models are more stable but are not as agile. You can even buy a kit to retrofit your old single-wheeled model with two additional back wheels, sure proof that those who spend too much time pushing around a wheelbarrow are bound to design a better version, if only for their own sake.

Garden carts are the big cousins of wheelbarrows. They are flat-bottomed, two-wheeled carts, capable of toting upwards of 800 pounds. Some are made to be pulled by lawn tractors, some by hand.

Lawn-Care Tools

Your main lawn-care investment is obviously your lawn mower, but you might need a few other tools to help control where and how your grass grows.

▶ **Edgers** make a clean cut at the border where grass meets another ground cover, such as pavement or planting beds. A sharp, half-moon-shaped head slices away sod. A sharp spade or garden knife does the same job.

▶ **Spreaders** apply fertilizer to lawns. You can buy a shoulder-carried version in which you turn a crank to spin granules out onto the lawn. But the more useful, and back-friendly, option is a hopper on wheels that you push. Most let you adjust the rate of application to your needs.

▶ **Weeders** come in a variety of types, from handheld models that pop weeds from the roots to rotating "twister" or "claw" models that twist weeds up from the soil, roots and all. A handheld ball weeder or a notched asparagus knife are useful for popping weeds out of the lawn without tearing up the turf. Some models are cleverly marketed for specific purposes, such as getting in between thickly planted perennials or popping weeds out of lawns without leaving divots. Some can even be attached to a drill to make the job easier.

Gas- and Electric- Powered Tools

Most power tools constitute a hefty initial investment, which must be worked off over a period of time. They also represent a monetary commitment to run; they require fuel or electricity, maintenance, and, occasionally, repairs. The trade-off is that they save time and effort.

Chippers and Shredders

Chippers and shredders reduce garden waste by three-quarters or more, a real boon if you cannot burn or haul yard waste to a landfill in your area. Shredders reduce twigs and leaves to fine mulch. Chippers/shredders also chop branches (up to 3 inches in diameter for most home models), making them more versatile. Both types speed up the process of composting. (See Chapter 6).

Electric units are quiet and spew no pollutants, but generally can't compare with the horse power of gas-powered models, so are most suited to small yards that produce little waste.

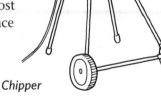

Chipper

Rototillers

Rototillers cultivate soil. Models range from 1-horsepower, lightweight tiller/cultivators designed mainly for mechanized weeding, to 14-horsepower tillers made for breaking new ground. Sharp digging tines rotate and cultivate the soil to depths varying from 4 to 8 inches.

Considering that most plant roots penetrate at least a foot deep, a rototiller alone cannot prepare the soil deeply enough to fully accommodate them.

The digging tines may be mounted in the front or rear of the machine. Except for the most powerful models, those designed with rear-mounted tines can be difficult to control at tilling depths greater than 3 inches. Rototillers can be dangerous; never buy one without a deadman control. This safety feature stops the machine and the turning tines when engaged.

Rototiller

String Trimmers

String trimmers cut unruly herbaceous growth, from weeds to overgrown grass. There are gas- and electric-powered models, but unless you have enough weeds to warrant the gas type, a good pair of garden shears will work instead. Some trimmers can also edge lawns; turn them so the string spins vertically.

String trimmer

Hedge Trimmers

Hedge trimmers are for yards with lots of big hedges. Gas-powered models are easy to use, are cordless, and have little vibration. But they are loud and expensive. Electric trimmers are cheaper and more lightweight. Those with reciprocating blades — two blades cutting against each other — are the most efficient. For most uses a 16-inch blade is sufficient.

Electric hedge trimmer

Leaf Blowers

In a large area a blower will save effort and time over a rake. There are hand-carried, backpack, and push types, some with attachments. They are loud and expensive, and they take all the fun out of raking leaves.

DIRT CHEAP

Push-reel mowers may seem like a relic, but for small, flat lawns there is no smarter alternative. Rotating blades cut grass evenly while providing a workout. Compared to motorized models, they are cheaper to purchase and to operate, the only cost being occasional sharpening of the blades. And they don't emit pollutants from burning fuel.

Waterworks

Watering equipment can be costly, but you may save in the long run by lowering your water bills or pumping costs. You have several options when it comes to delivering water to your lawn and garden.

Garden Hoses

Garden hoses vary in length and can be screwed together to cover long distances. Rubber and vinyl hoses are the most common, and are available in ½-inch, ⅝-inch, ¾-inch, and 1-inch diameters. For most uses a ⅝-inch size is the best buy, and rubber lasts the longest and is least prone to kinking and splitting. Look for hoses with a lifetime guarantee. Hoses go on sale in spring and fall.

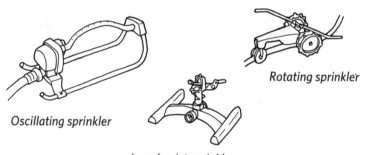

Oscillating sprinkler

Impulse-jet sprinkler

Rotating sprinkler

Rotating and pulse-jet sprinklers have moving parts that deliver an even spray. Impulse-jet types are the most versatile, because you can adjust them to water a range of patterns, including a full circle. Oscillating sprinklers have a rocking bar that sprays water.

Lawn Sprinklers

Lawn sprinklers are not the best choice for vegetable plots, flower borders, or landscaping plants, because so much water lands on foliage instead of near the roots. If you must use a sprinkler in these spots, elevate it with a stepladder or other substitute so the spray lands unobstructed. A lot of it still winds up on foliage, but won't be completely blocked from one plant by the leaves of another as often happens at ground level. Look for sales of sprinklers in spring and fall.

The cheapest sprinklers cost between $5 and $8 and have small heads with holes punched in them. They rest on the ground and shoot water up over a limited area. These work all right for lawns, but in a border or vegetable garden the spray may be blocked by foliage.

Drip Irrigation Systems

In-ground systems deliver water through emitters to individual plants. They are great for putting just the right amount of water where needed but can be costly to install. A less expensive option is a system of soaker or porous hoses that deliver water along their length either through a series of holes or through the porous skin.

Some soaker hoses can be used to water lawns, as the holes are large enough to send water spraying upward, covering more ground. Turn them over so the water sprays downward to water vegetables or flowers. These hoses conserve water by putting it only where desired. Place one along each garden row or wind a few through flower beds and landscaping, to save time moving them around.

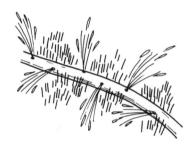

A soaker hose will help you save significantly on your water bill. It can be adjusted to spray upward or downward.

Sometimes the simplest tools are the handiest. Knives, for example, have many uses in the garden. Use them for pruning, taking cuttings, grafting, and harvesting. A good pocketknife with a sharp, carbon steel blade is a fine investment. A pair of heavy shears is another good choice for trimming hedges, snipping grass, cutting back perennials, or creating topiary master-pieces. Look for those with straight, sharp blades on sturdy wooden handles.

GREEN THUMB

Keeping an Eye on the Time

Save time and money by using automatic timers that shut the water off at a predetermined time. Cheap ones simply turn it off after a preset time period, but you can program expensive computer models with a complete watering regime. Both models prevent waste from overwatering, but the less expensive mechanical type is simpler to use and should be sufficient for almost anyone. Be careful where you place them, as direct sun will render some models useless. Freezing temperatures will also damage the working parts so bring them in before frost.

Electronic timer

To determine how long to water a particular spot, use a water gauge to measure how much water lands there over a period of time. You don't need to buy one; just place an empty jar or can in the areas you want to measure. Either mark the sides of the jar with a permanent marker or measure the depth of water periodically with a ruler.

Mechanical timer

DIRT CHEAP

A soaker hose is a bigger initial expense than a garden hose or cheap sprinkler, but the savings on water will pay for the added investment. Soaker hoses also last longer, having no moving parts to break or jam.

Comforts and Conveniences

There are a few items that no gardener should step outside without.

▶ **Cheap cloth gloves** keep your hands clean. Heavy-duty leather gloves protect against thorns during pruning or brush cutting and guard against blisters after hours of hoeing or spading.

▶ **A hat** protects you from overheating and sun exposure, and spares your eyes the strain of squinting on bright days.

▶ **Handle grips** reduce wear on both handles and hands. For a cheap substitute wrap handles with foam pipe insulation, attached neatly with electrical tape.

▶ **Kneepads and kneelers** help prevent aches from hours of weeding or digging. Kneepads allow more free movement than a kneeler that must be picked up and moved every few minutes as you change position.

DIRT CHEAP

Use an old, plastic laundry basket, a five-gallon bucket, or an old canvas tote bag when weeding, as a more portable alternative to a wheelbarrow.

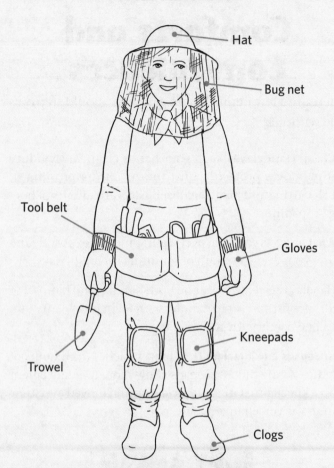

Hat

Bug net

Tool belt

Gloves

Trowel

Kneepads

Clogs

The Hardy Gardener

While having the proper gear makes gardening more enjoyable, most gardeners don't need to suit up this completely for an hour of weeding — with this outfit, you could go on safari!

Planting Aids

From starting seeds to maintaining full-grown plants, there is equipment for every step of the way. Almost anything you can buy for those jobs has a free or cheap substitute, if you even need it all. **Soil thermometers,** for instance, can help you decide when to seed temperature-sensitive plants. However, with practice, and perhaps a little trial and error, you'll soon develop a "feel" for soil temperature that's just as dependable. For an experienced gardener, it's enough to know if it's warm enough to plant.

Seed-starting pots are available in plastic or peat, but there is no reason to pay for them — see chapter 5 for alternatives. Save pots and flats whenever you purchase plants and reuse them.

Labels are easily made by cutting waxed milk cartons into strips and writing on the plain side with a permanent marker; just push them an inch or two into the ground near the plants. Or push a stick through the top of seed packets and out the bottom to make custom stakes to mark rows.

MORE

DIRT CHEAP

Instead of buying special plant ties, use cloth strips, plastic garbage-bag ties, twine, or twist ties. Wire tomato cages make great supports for many flowering plants; you can cut them down to size with wire snips or even cut them in half to make two.

For larger plants and vining crops, welded-wire fencing, hopefully salvaged, makes a good support, as do rustic-looking wooden cages built of salvaged 1 × 2s.

Metal fence posts are available in various lengths, are reasonably priced, will last forever, and will support the weight of any crop. Since metal heats up in the sun, avoid training vines directly up the posts, or else wrap the post in decorative cloth strips or twine to give tender plant tendrils a break.

Proper Care for Longer Wear

The secret to protecting your investment in garden tools and equipment is taking good care of what you buy. Most importantly, clean all tools immediately after use, and store them out of the weather.

Pruners, Loppers, and Shears

The first rule is never misuse these cutting tools. They are meant to cut stems, not branches, wire, or bolts. One wrong cut can ruin a good blade. Use soap and water to wash away sap or pitch; you may need a bit of turpentine or hand cleaner for particularly sticky spots. Scrub with steel wool to remove rust, and keep the moving parts lubricated with WD-40 or sewing machine oil. Check nuts and bolts periodically

Keep your digging tools shipshape by hosing off dirt after each use and then plunging the tool into a bucket of oily sand a few times. The sand scours the metal as the oil coats it, helping to prevent rust. After a good plunge, hang up the tool in its proper spot. Mix a bottle of vegetable oil with enough clean construction sand to dampen the sand. (Don't use motor oil; it can introduce petrochemicals into your soil.) You'll need to remix the oil and sand periodically to keep the oil from settling to the bottom.

GREEN THUMB

to make sure they are tight. Sharpen if cutting becomes difficult.

Digging Tools

Coat wooden handles with varnish or rub with linseed or tung oil at the end of the season to preserve the grain. All your tools will perform better if the edge is sharp. File tools to a sharp edge at least once a year (see page 75).

Power Equipment

The best advice is to follow the manufacturer's maintenance recommendations. Use only recommended fuel, change oil and filters on schedule, monitor spark plugs on gas models, and keep all blades sharp. Remove any debris from chippers, shredders, and lawn mowers before storing. Drain fuel before putting away for the winter.

DIRT CHEAP

Proper maintenance goes a long way toward preventing premature tool damage. Eventually, something is bound to break, get stuck, or become dull. Knowing how and when to repair rather than replace is important for the frugal gardener. If you correct a small problem immediately, it won't become a big problem. Some items require repairs beyond the average gardener's ability but still don't need to be replaced. Take mowers, tillers, shredders, and trimmers to a professional for repairs. If you attempt to fix the machine, it could void your warranty, take a lot of time, and possibly ruin your equipment.

Getting a Grip

You can extend the life of any wooden handle the day you buy it. Use fine sandpaper to remove the finish. With your bare hands or a soft rag, generously rub the handle with boiled, cooled linseed oil. The warmth from your hands will help work in the oil, or leave a rag-oiled handle in the sun for a few hours. Tung oil or vegetable oils such as olive or safflower oils also make good preservatives. The result is a smooth, water-resistant finish. Replenish with another rub whenever the wood begins to lose its satiny feel.

Replacing Handles

Replace cracked shovel or fork handles promptly. Resist the temptation to "get by" with a broken handle. Digging puts a lot of stress on these tools, and having one give out at the wrong moment can be dangerous.

To be sure you buy the proper-sized replacement handle, take the old tool with you to the hardware store. There are almost more handle sizes and variations than there are tools.

MORE ▶

DIRT CHEAP

Don't try to get by with wrapping tape around a cracked handle. It may be thrifty, but it only hides a potentially dangerous problem. A new handle is cheaper than a visit to the emergency room.

Nothing wastes more time and money than having to go back and forth attempting to replace something you were trying to be cheap about in the first place.

1. Take the screw or rivet out of the tool socket carefully, without altering the socket shape. If it is wedged in tight, you may have to tap the handle loose. Pick any splinters or debris out of the socket.

2. Secure the tool head in a vise and push the handle into the socket. A little oil or soap will help the handle slide in easily, especially with curved sockets. Tap the handle in as far as it will go.

3. Prevent the new handle from ever flying free by drilling a hole and inserting a nut and bolt through the metal socket into the handle.

A Fix for Hoses

My hoses seem to get shorter every year. That's because rather than throw them away after accidentally smashing the couplings or cutting them in half, I repair them. There are two types of repair kits, which differ in how you secure the coupling. One type uses prongs that clamp down around the end of the hose, and the other applies a band at the hose end.

Before using either type of kit, first cut away the damaged coupling or shredded section of hose, then soak the hose end in hot water for a few minutes to soften.

Staying Sharp

Sharpening equipment properly is a refined skill. You will need a vise, a file or whetstone, and a basic understanding of the function of the edge that you are sharpening. If you're not comfortable sharpening your own tools, it's worth the investment to have it done professionally. Maintenance is almost always cheaper than replacement!

Sharpening is not always the answer, however. Large nicks in any blade mean it's time for a replacement. On better pruners and loppers, you can adjust the anvils to make up for wear on the blades. Make sure the nut or bolt is tight.

Shovels, spades, and **hoes** get dull from digging through rocks. To sharpen, secure the head in a vise, don a pair of gloves, and grasp the file at both ends. A 10-inch mill bastard file works best. Run the file along the beveled rim of the shovel, applying force as you push forward and lifting up as you pull back. Only sharpen the beveled side.

The angle between the file and the head determines how strong or sharp the finished edge will be; a wider angle gives a stronger edge, and a narrow angle results in a sharper edge. Many gardeners prefer a strong edge on shovels and a slicing one on hoes, but a 35- to 40-degree angle yields a sturdy, sharp blade.

Sharpen **pruners** or **shears** with a small, flat, single-cut file or whetstone. Secure one handle in the vise, and apply force only with the angle of the blades. Push the file from the hinged part of the blade to the tip. Never file along the flat side of bypass or parrot-bill shears. The clean cut made by these pruners is the direct result of the beveled edge gliding closely along the flat; altering the flat side leaves a gap.

Lawn mower blades should be sharpened once a year. To sharpen, remove blades if possible, or disconnect the spark plug wire for safety's sake if sharpening on the mower. Using a bastard file, draw along the edge on either side, filing equally on each side to maintain balance.

Sharpening your shovels will make them last longer and perform more effectively.

You Can Rent Nearly Anything

When considering adding tools to your gardening ensemble, take a hard look at how often you will use a new piece of equipment. If, like a heavy-duty rototiller, it will only see action a couple of times a year, think about renting one only when you need it. True, it is less convenient to pick it up, lug it home, and return it after use. But there are no maintenance costs, no storage hassles, and no parting with the purchase price.

One Big Caveat

Keep in mind that you are charged for the entire time you have the machine, not just for the time you actually use it. Do all your prep work *before* your trip to the rental store. Nothing is a more frustrating waste of money than having a $40 an hour machine sitting idle while you tear down a section of garden fence you forgot about, haul out rocks, and pull out last year's row markers.

Neighborly cooperation can save you even more money. Arrange a mutual rental/work weekend with a gardening friend to save expenses and help each other get your work done faster.

The Most Precious Resource

Your gardening community provides not only a useful resource but also a lot of fun. Whether your friends and neighbors are next door, miles away, or connected by the Internet, take advantage of the knowledge, goodwill, and stuff that other people have to offer (see Resources).

Another way you can benefit one another is through buying power. Buy in bulk and save big bucks. A bale of potting soil, as compared to the relatively tiny prepacked bags will last a dozen people all spring at a fraction of the cost. One thousand plastic plant markers will last forever and cost next to nothing if split among a group.

The more ways you find to help yourself through helping others, the bigger and better your gardening community will become.

CHAPTER 3

PRICELESS PLANTS

Let's take a look at your plant budget. What plant budget, you ask? Setting a limit on spending somehow seems ungardener-like. Most gardeners always seem to scrape up enough cash or credit to buy just one more interesting plant or just a few more packets of unusual seeds. Wouldn't it be nice if you could cut your costs but still have all the plants you want? Here are some ways to do just that.

Free Seeds

Compared to the overall cost of gardening, seeds are a real bargain. But why pay for them when they are all around you for free? If you have plants, you have seeds. You should know, however, that seeds from hybrid plants don't produce plants just like their parents. If you plan to collect seed for future plantings, you will have better results if you choose seeds or plants that are labeled "open pollinated" (OP) in a catalog or at a nursery.

Saving Your Own Seeds

Before any plant can set seed, it must be pollinated. Some are self-pollinating, which means the flowers on the plant produce and accept their own pollen. Others require pollen from a second plant, delivered either by the breeze or the bees.

The easiest plants from which to successfully save seed are self-pollinated annuals. They are the most reliable in producing plants with identical traits to the parent plant, such as taste, texture, color, bloom time, and so on. Many perennials are also easy to propagate from seed. Biennials don't flower or set seed until their second year, so they often require protection over the winter to stay alive long enough to yield seed.

DiRT CHEAP

Collect seeds only from your sturdiest and healthiest garden plants. Never collect seed from diseased plants, because some diseases are seed borne.

Growing conditions during seed development affect the quality of seeds, so take good care of the expectant plants. Choose the very best example of each type of plant as the parent for the next generation. Look for early production; plant vigor; good color; fine flavor; superior size, texture, or yield; and disease and insect resistance. For plants such as spinach that must sacrifice the harvestable part of the plant to set seed, collect seed from those that produce the longest, not those that bolt first.

GREEN THUMB

▶ **Step 1:** Let one or more plants of a chosen variety go to seed. First the plant must flower, and then fruit, such as a tomato, a peapod, a rosehip, an apple, or a seed head will form. Leave the fruit on the plant until it is past ripe or about to fall off.

▶ **Step 2:** Pick fruit or seed head. Remove seeds and separate out all non-seed material (it can harbor moisture that will affect the storage life of seeds).

▶ **Step 3:** Air-dry seeds thoroughly before packaging in envelopes or airtight containers.

▶ **Step 4:** Label and store seeds in a cool, dry place.

▶ **Step 5:** When ready to use, test seeds for germination. (See page 88.)

▶ **Step 6:** Sow.

Preventing Unwanted Pollination

In the garden, usually only plants of the same species can cross-pollinate. Even though you will lose certain traits — such as color, texture, sweetness, or flavor — a cross between two types, say of broccoli or carrots, usually doesn't result in any tremendous surprises. But let pumpkins, squashes, and some gourds mingle, and you could find some real oddballs in next year's pumpkin patch.

When you are planning to save seeds, you may want to prevent cross-pollination of crops such as broccoli by covering them with cheesecloth. This keeps the insects away but requires that you then pollinate plants by hand.

The trick, then, is finding a way to prevent pollen from one plant from landing on the flowers of another variety. There are four ways to do this:

▶ Use a physical barrier to separate or cover the plants.

▶ Space different varieties far apart.

▶ Grow varieties that flower at different times.

▶ Plant only one variety of a plant per season.

DIRT CHEAP

Join a seed exchange or start your own with some friends and neighbors. Over time you will store up enough seed so that you can plant multiple varieties some years and still have seed left over to plant a single variety for collection the following season. Remember, seeds last for years, so you won't need to save seed of every type of plant every year.

Plants Suitable for Seed Saving

Wind-Pollinated Vegetables

Beet (b)

Corn (a)

Spinach (a)

Swiss chard (b)

Insect-Pollinated Vegetables

Asparagus (p)

Broccoli (a, b)

Brussels sprouts (b)

Cabbage (b)

Carrot (b)

Cauliflower (a,b)

Celeriac (b)

Celery (b)

Chinese cabbage (b)

Collards (b)

Cucumber (a)

Eggplant (a)

Kale (b)

Kohlrabi (b)

Melon (a)

Onion (b)

Parsley (b)

Parsnip (b)

Peppers (a)

Pumpkin (a)

Radish (b)

Rutabaga (b)

Squash (a)

Turnip (b)

Self-Pollinated Vegetables

Beans (a)

Endive (a)

Lettuce (a)

Peas (a)*

Tomatillo (a)

Tomato (a)

Flowers

Calendula (a)

Cleome (a)

Columbine (p)

Datura (a)

Foxglove (a)

Hollyhock (a)

Larkspur (a)

Marigold (a)

Morning glory (a)

Nasturtium (a)

Poppy (a)

Snapdragon (a)

Sweet pea (a)

Zinnia (a)

*Peas are self-fertile, but separate different varieties by 50 feet to ensure purity of seed.

KEY: (a) = annual, (b) = biennial, (p) = perennial

Collecting Seeds

Once you have seeds, the next step is to gather and prepare them for storage. For most plants, it is critical to wait until the seeds are fully ripe before you harvest them. This generally means that the fruit itself will be overripe, but failure to wait results in seeds with a low germination rate and poor vigor.

Some exceptions are snap beans, lettuce, radishes, spinach, and tomatoes, which germinate fairly well when a little underripe. Although the seeds must be ripe, it also is important to make sure they are not yet rotten or expelled by the plant when harvesting. A dry, sunny day is perfect for gathering seeds or seed fruit. The method of harvest depends on the type of plant:

▶ **Small seeds:** Many annual flowers, lettuce, and onions release their seeds as soon as they mature. Tie a small paper bag over the developing seed head to catch them as they fall.

▶ **Large seeds:** Some plants produce seedpods; snap them off, break open, and shake the seeds out over white paper to dry.

▶ **Fruits:** Wait until fleshy fruits, such as melons, tomatoes, shrub berries, or tree fruit, are a little overripe before you pick them. Scrape the seeds from the flesh, soak to remove any residue, and allow to dry completely.

MORE ▶

How to Collect Flower Seed

The toughest part is letting your best blossoms go to seed. Some flowers, such as marigolds, will hold their seeds right in the blossom; others will set a "fruit" or "pod" of some form. You can cut flower stalks as the seed heads start to split, then hang them upside down in a paper bag to dry; the seeds will drop to the bottom of the bag. Some flower seeds are tough to separate from the seed head — rubbing them against a piece of screen will help dislodge the seeds and save your fingers.

The moisture content of stored seeds is critical to their viability. (Viability determines whether or not it will sprout.) Seeds must be kept as dry as possible. Spread clean seeds out on newspapers in a dry, breeze-free place for at least one week. Hang an incandescent lightbulb overhead to raise the temperature slightly and dry the surrounding air. Temperatures much over 100°F (37.8°C) as well as any other factors causing the seeds to dry too quickly will damage them.

Some seeds will dry just fine on the plant; poppy seeds and peas are good examples. An alternate method is wrapping the seeds in paper and placing them in a jar with an equal weight of silica gel. Small seeds will dry in about 10 days, while larger ones can take up to 16 days. Test for dryness by bending the seeds. Those that snap back are not ready for storage, but those that break are ready.

Storing Seeds

The storage life of your saved seed depends on the type and quality of the seeds, how well they survive drying, and the storage environment. The longer you store seeds, the less viable and vigorous they will be. Commercially packed seed may store longer than homegrown, but virtually all seeds will retain some degree of viability long after the best germination rates have passed.

Seeds must be kept dry and cool, otherwise they rot or sprout. Humidity between 20 and 40 percent (seed moisture content between 5 and 8 percent) and temperatures between 32 and 41°F (0 and 5°C) are ideal. Add a packet of desiccant powder (such as silica gel) or powdered milk to combat high humidity. The gel absorbs best.

Never throw away old seed without first testing to see if it will sprout. I once found some old tomato seeds of a favorite variety that were 18 years old. I thought there was no way they would sprout, but of course, I tested them anyway. Out of the dozen or so seeds left at the bottom of the packet, 10 healthy plants developed. It always pays to be cheap.

Testing Stored Seeds

Faster germination results in more vigorous plants. To determine how well your seeds have survived storage, perform a germination test. You are looking for a high percentage of the seeds to sprout within the normal time for the plant's type.

- Moisten a paper towel or coffee filter.
- Place ten or twenty seeds on it.
- Fold in half or quarters.
- Seal in a ziplock plastic bag. (You can place several "test papers" in one bag.)
- Open daily to check for germination.
- After the appropriate amount of time has passed for that type of seed, count the number of sprouts to figure the percentage.

Five out of 10 seeds and 10 out of 20 seeds gives a 50 percent rate. More seeds in the test will yield more accurate results. An over 60 percent germination rate is good, better than 70 percent is average, and better than 90 percent is great. The fewer seeds that germinate in your test, the more you will need to plant to compensate. If you know that only about half your seeds will come up, you'll need to put twice as many in the ground at planting time to get the same number of plants as for seeds with 90% viability. Of course the viability of seed varies with the age of the seed, the conditions under which is has been stored, and the plant/variety of seed itself.

Hurray for Self-Sowers

Some plants just won't give you the satisfaction of saving and using your own seed. They are do-it-yourselfers, or self-sowers. If you don't pluck every last spent blossom from plants such as calendula, French marigolds, forget-me-nots, and sweet alyssum, they will seed themselves back. Personally, I like this approach. You not only save money but also time and effort.

Since only open-pollinated varieties will grow true from seed, some second-generation flowers won't grow up to look just like their parents, which is fine as long as they produce interesting or attractive plants. When you are weeding in the spring, look for familiar seedlings, lest you accidentally cull volunteer flowers (self-sown plants that pop up unexpectedly). Here's a list of well-known self-sowers:

Calendula	Forget-me-not	Nasturtium
California poppy	Four o'clock	Nicotiana
Cleome (spider flower)	Foxglove	Pansy
Coreopsis	French marigold	Poppy
Cornflower	Gloriosa daisy	Snapdragon
Corydalis	Godetia	Sweet alyssum
Cosmos	Larkspur	Sweet pea
Dill	Love-in-a-mist	Violet
Flax	Morning glory	

Seedy Deals

Mail-order catalogs and display racks everywhere from garden centers to grocery and hardware stores sell seeds. Which sources offer the best bargains?

▶ **Mail-Order Seed Companies:** Compare several catalogs, and you will quickly find that most are selling the same seeds, packaged a little differently, in a range of prices. Look for the best-priced varieties having traits you desire.

▶ **Seed Exchanges:** You can find these useful resources online or in gardening magazines. These are a great way to get seeds, often of rare or heirloom varieties that are hard to find elsewhere.

▶ **Plant Associations:** Fan clubs abound for nearly every kind of plant from alpines to zinnias. National groups usually maintain a Web site or send out a newsletter in which members list plants they have to offer. If you have a real passion for a particular kind of plant, join the local chapter of the appropriate association. (Of course, the *really cheap* way is to become friends with someone who is already a member and borrow a copy of his or her newsletter!)

DIRT CHEAP

Seed companies only sell seed packaged for the current year. At the end of each season, you can get megabargains on this year's product. Seeds that cost $2.50 a packet in the spring may be priced at 10 packets for $1.00 when the stores are clearing inventory. Garden centers offer the least drastic discounts, while grocery stores, hardware stores, and other stores not normally in the garden-supply business just want to get rid of them.

Buy discounted seeds at the end of the season to save for the following year. A word of caution, however: Remember that the perfect environment for storing seed is a cool, dry place. Don't buy from seed racks exposed to rain or excess summer heat. The seed may already be ruined.

Whenever possible, I prefer to buy from local companies. For one thing, the biggest company doesn't necessarily offer the smallest price. Furthermore, small seed companies often focus on local conditions and offer varieties that will thrive in your immediate area.

Plant Parenthood

For many types of plants, there are faster, more inexpensive ways to cultivate new specimens than waiting for seeds to form and grow. Vegetative propagation means starting a new plant from an appropriate piece of an old one. Several methods exist, including taking cuttings, layering, dividing, and separating bulbs.

A Cut Above

You can take cuttings from the stem, leaves, or roots of various plant species. Often one method works better than the others for a specific plant; even varieties within a species respond differently. Some plants root more easily than others. If a cutting doesn't root well in the spring, try again later

DIRT CHEAP

Creating free plants by taking cuttings is a method well suited to houseplants, many of which readily form roots from stems stuck in a jar of water. With some species, such as African violets and most succulents, you'll have better luck making leaf cuttings. In this case, roots form along the veins, and usually several new plantlets emerge from each leaf cutting. If you master the art of taking stem and leaf cuttings, you may find yourself suddenly surrounded by new plants. If you're being overrun, pot up a few in attractive containers (clean, recycled terra cotta pots are a good choice) for thoughtful gifts.

in the season. Since plants mature at different rates, in different climes, and even in different years, there always will be some variability. Keep records to refine the practice for your area.

How to Take Stem Cuttings

▶ **Step 1:** Use a sharp knife or scissors to ensure a clean cut, and choose a healthy stem, preferably without flowers. Slicing at an angle (to increase rooting surface area), cut the stem of the parent plant approximately 1 inch beneath a node.

▶ **Step 2:** If you must transport the cutting, gently wrap it in a moistened, absorbent paper towel and put it in a plastic bag.

▶ **Step 3:** Often you can take several cuttings from each collected stem. Make each cutting 3 or 4 inches long. Trim the end of each stem to just below a node, and strip off any leaves below it. Snip off any flowers and all but two or three leaves above the node.

▶ **Step 4:** Dip in rooting hormone, if desired, to boost root-cell division. Commercial products are made from synthetic plant hormones (usually indolebutyric acid, or IBA).

▶ **Step 5:** Gently push cuttings into moist rooting medium, angled end first, about an inch deep. A sterile, soilless mix works best. (Some plants, such as pelargonium and coleus, will root in a glass of water. Adding a pinch of rooting powder to the water speeds the process.)

▶ **Step 6:** Cover cuttings with plastic to keep them moist, and keep warm (room temperature). Be sure to ventilate for air circulation by removing the plastic two or three times a day to allow fresh air under the plastic or by cutting slits in the plastic.

As soon as roots start to develop (you can test by gently tugging on a cutting to see if it resists), increase the ventilation to lower the humidity. Keep in a bright, well-lit area but out of direct sunlight.

▶ **Step 7:** Pot or transplant cuttings when new growth shows, in four to six weeks.

How to Take Leaf Cuttings

▶ **Step 1:** Cut a healthy leaf from the parent plant.

▶ **Step 2:** Place it in moist rooting medium. The leaf may be set upright so the blade is in contact with the rooting medium (A). You also can cut several nicks along the length of the veins, and press the leaf flat-vein-side down in the rooting medium (B). Or cut the leaf lengthwise and insert into rooting medium with the cut side down to expose the veins (C).

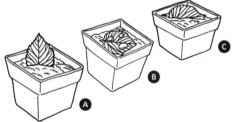

Three methods of planting a leaf cutting.

▶ **Step 3:** Cover with clear plastic, and place in a warm area away from direct sunlight.

▶ **Step 4:** Keep the rooting medium moist.

▶ **Step 5:** Pot new plants after a few leaves appear.

Plants Suitable for Leaf Cuttings

African violet	Christmas cactus	Gloxinia	Peperomia
Begonia	Echevaria	Hen and chicks	Sedum
Cape primrose		Jade plant	

You can take cuttings from the stems of many plant species, using one of the following methods: softwood, semi-hardwood, or hardwood. For detailed instructions, consult a good reference book or online site (see Resources for suggestions).

Plants Suitable for Softwood Stem Cuttings

Softwood cuttings are taken from the current season's growth, before it begins to harden, which is usually May through July in most areas. Stems suitable for softwood cuttings have a mix of both small young and full-sized mature leaves, and they snap easily if bent. They are the easiest to root, but fragile and prone to drying out.

Fruit

Blueberry	Elderberry	Plum
Cherry	Fig	Serviceberry
Crabapple	Grape	

Perennials*

Delphinium	Hibiscus	Primula
Dianthus	Lupine	Verbena
Fuchsia	Phlox	Viola

Climbers

Blackeyed susan vine	English ivy	Ivy geranium
Clematis, some	Glorybower	Morning glory
Climbing hydrangea	Honeysuckle	Trumpet vine (various species)

Take stem cuttings whenever shoots are available.

Shrubs

Barberry	Forsythia	Mock orange
Beautybush	Fuchsia	Potentilla
Boxwood	Heath	Redtwig dogwood
Butterfly bush	Hydrangea	Rose
Camellia	Japanese maple	Spirea
Cotoneaster	Kerria	Viburnum
Daphne	Lantana	Weigela
Euonymus (burning bush)	Lilac	Wintercreeper
Flowering quince	Magnolia	Witch hazel

Plants Suitable for Semi-Hardwood Stem Cuttings

Semi-hardwood cuttings are taken in the summer before the stems have fully matured, usually midsummer to early fall. Stems sport fully developed leaves and the wood is fairly well hardened. These cuttings root a little slower than spring cuttings but on average are more likely to survive.

Climbers

Clematis, some varieties
Grapes, some varieties
Honeysuckle
Trumpet vine

Perennials

Daphne
Geranium
Helianthemum
Veronica

Shrubs

Bottlebrush
Camellia
Cotoneaster
Daphne
Holly
Oregon grape
Rhododendron
Rose
Rose of Sharon
Viburnum
Weigela

Trees

Arborvitae
Cedar
Cypress
False cypress
Hemlock
Holly
Juniper
Magnolia

Plants Suitable for Hardwood Stem Cuttings

Hardwood cuttings are taken from dormant, mature stems after the growing season, late fall through early spring. Stems are hard and will not bend easily, leaves may be absent. They are usually the slowest to root.

Climbers
Bougainvillea
Hardy kiwi
Honeysuckle (some varieties)
Virginia creeper

Fruit
Blueberry (some varieties)
Currant
Fig
Gooseberry
Grape
Raspberry

Shrubs
Boxwood
Butterfly bush
Cotoneaster
Dogwood
Elderberry
Forsythia
Japanese aucuba
Mock orange
Rosa rugosa
Spirea
Viburnum
Weigela

Trees
Dawn redwood
Ficus
Mulberry
Poplar
Sycamore
Willow

DIRT CHEAP

You can make your own rooting hormone from a natural source by cutting willow twigs several inches long, slicing the bark to allow the hormone to leach out, and steeping them in water for a day or two. Use the willow water to soak cuttings before placing them in growing medium, to water newly rooted cuttings or transplants.

Rooting for New Plants

Some plants readily sprout new individuals from pieces of root. A lot of weeds come to mind, but you can use this method to propagate some of your garden favorites as well. All you need is the proper type of plant, a sharp knife, some moist growing medium, and a little bit of time.

How to Take Root Cuttings

▶ **Step 1:** Gently dig through the soil to expose young, growing roots, approximately pencil-sized. Herbaceous perennials may be thinner.

▶ **Step 2:** With a sharp knife cut the root straight across, and place an angled cut farther down the root. This way you can tell which end is up.

▶ **Step 3:** If you must transport the cutting, wrap it in a moist paper towel.

▶ **Step 4:** Remove any fibrous roots. You can divide long cuttings and shorten thinner ones to between 3 and 5 inches. Make a fresh, slanted cut in each piece to designate top and bottom.

▶ **Step 5:** Dip cutting into rooting hormone.

MORE

▶ **Step 6:** Insert cutting into moist rooting medium with the slanted end down and the straight-cut end level with the surface. Lay thin roots sideways, and cover lightly with soil. You can root some species, such as lilac and sumac, directly into the garden site.

▶ **Step 7:** Pot or transplant roots after a few leaves develop.

Plants Suitable for Taking Root Cuttings

Perennials

Bellflower

Blanket flower

Bluebell

Creeping phlox

Cupid's dart

Geranium, some varieties

Globeflower

Japanese anemone

Oriental poppy

Phlox

Shrubs, Trees, and Vines

Blackberry (vine)

Crabapple (tree)

Fig

Glorybower

Lilac

Pacific wax myrtle

Raspberry (vine)

Rose

Sumac

Trumpet vine

New Plants from Layering

Layering stems to produce new plants is almost too easy. It works best with plants that have vining or flexible stems. By either covering a section of stem with soil or simulating that effect, the stem sprouts roots. Once rooted, the stem can be separated from the parent plant and transplanted.

Simple Layering

This method works best during the plant's dormant season. Cut a small nick into the bottom side of a stem, and anchor it into prepared soil, either on the ground or in a pot. It helps to stake the tip of the stem. Leave it alone, except to water, until the end of the next growing season. If the roots are strong, then cut the new plant from the parent and transplant. Plants such as forsythia, honeysuckle, rhododendron, and roses respond well to this technique.

Tip layering works particularly well with raspberry and blackberry varieties. It works like simple layering, except you bury the tip of the vine. Serpentine layering involves anchoring a long stem to the soil in several spots. It's a great way to make several copies of plants, such as clematis or climbing roses, that send out long, flexible stems.

MORE

Air Layering

With this technique you trick the stem into believing it has been anchored in the soil. It works well with citrus trees, magnolias, and mountain laurels.

Step 1: Remove any leaves that are in the way. Make a sleeve from plastic wrap, and fit it over or around the stem; wrap the bottom with tape. Make a slanted cut upward into the stem with a sharp knife.

Step 2: Quickly pack moist sphagnum moss around the stem and into the cut using the back of the knife.

Step 3: Pull the sleeve up, pack fully with more damp moss, and seal the top of the plastic sleeve firmly with tape.

Step 4: Eventually roots will show through the plastic. At this point, cut the stem off just below the new root ball and pot up the new plant.

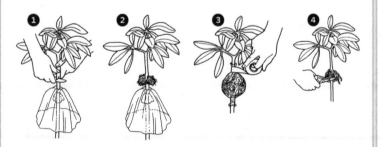

Divide and Multiply

Dividing is a quick way to increase your collection of perennials, succulents, and some houseplants and suckering shrubs, and it is healthier for the original plant than being left to overcrowd itself.

GREEN THUMB

The best time to divide most plants is from late fall to early spring, when the plant is dormant. Avoid especially cold or wet periods, as these make it tough for the divided plants to reestablish. Plants with fleshy roots, such as irises, peonies, and poppies, have a better chance of rooting if divided in late summer.

Begin by gently digging around the base of the plant to expose the perimeters of it. Then carefully lift the plant with a garden fork. Shake or brush off as much soil as possible so you can see what you are doing. Often with older plants there will be a dead spot of brown stems in the center of the plant. Cut this out, and divide the remaining growth.

The simplest way to divide most plants is to grasp large sections by hand and gently, but firmly, pull them apart. Plants that can't be pulled apart can be cut through with a sharp spade. Make sure you leave a few buds on each division.

Cut back the tops, and place the new plants in the ground at the same height they were growing before, then water.

Bulbs, Corms, and Tubers

Bulbs, corms, and tubers are underground plant parts used to store energy for the coming year.

▶ **Bulbs** are made up of layers of modified leaves. There are two types, tunicate (or laminate), such as daffodils and tulips, and nontunicate (or scaly), such as lilies. Small bulbs form at the base of the plant, along the stem or roots. Reap the bounty of tiny bulbs by lifting a clump with a fork and carefully pulling the bulblets free. Pot them, and let them grow for a year or two before planting outside.

▶ **Corms** appear similar to bulbs, though they are solid rather than being made up of layers. You can separate them the same way, pulling young cormels away from the original

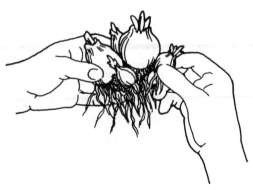

Bulb offsets can be separated and planted individually.

plant and either potting them up or planting them directly in a spot in the garden with good friable loam. They take a year or two to mature and flower. Gladiolus, crocus, freesia, cyclamen, and liatris are examples.

▶ **Tubers** are fleshy, modified underground stems or roots. Underground stem tubers include caladium and tuberous begonia. Root tubers include sweet potatoes and dahlias. In most parts of the country, you must dig them up every fall and bring them in from the cold. In the spring, as buds form, cut the tuber into sections with a couple of buds on each section.

DIRT CHEAP

One of the best reasons to belong to a garden club, apart from the friendship, is that members give each other or sell cheaply perfectly good plants. Plant swaps or sales are standard among clubs and are a great way to increase your plant collection. If you're not a member of a formal club, create the same opportunities simply by talking with others about your garden and theirs.

Landscape companies frequently redesign existing plantings, both residential and commercial. Construction firms remove existing plants every day when expanding structures, usually with a bulldozer. If you make contact with these people and offer to remove unwanted plants for free, you may find yourself with more plants than you can handle.

When You've Got to Spend

It's wonderful to get plants for free, but one of the joys of gardening is browsing through your favorite local nurseries for new varieties and great bargains. To score top-quality plants from your local garden center or nursery, cultivate the people who work there. They know the quality of their products, their wholesalers, when the plants arrived, how they were cared for, and any problems that may exist. Do yourself a favor; develop a relationship with these folks.

Know When to Shop

Plants arrive at the garden center from the supplier in the best possible condition, given the rigors of shipment. They sometimes go downhill from there. When scouting for plants, call and ask when the store expects to receive their shipment from their best supplier, and show up when the plants arrive. Not only will you get the healthiest possible plants, but you will also get first pick.

Signs of a Good Investment

Nurserymen know that blossoms attract buyers. Yet plants that have been forced into early bloom in order to make them more tempting to buyers can actually result in less productive plants in the long run. The stress of life with few roots and a big head slows plant vigor. Here's what to keep in mind when shopping:

▶ Look for compact, vigorous plants with healthy leaves.

▶ If you can find plants that are not yet in bloom, consider them first.

▶ Check the roots: Well-rooted plants recover from transplant shock more quickly and will live to bloom for years to come.

▶ Never buy sick or infested plants at any price.

DIRT CHEAP

You won't always get a bargain if you wait for plants to go on sale. If a plant has been sitting on a rack for months, especially if it doesn't receive proper care, then it probably won't amount to much. The best bets among such plants are perennials but only if the price is *really low*. If you feel you can bring a plant around, then by all means take a cheap gamble. Otherwise, spend wisely, and buy early.

CHAPTER 4

WINNING VARIETIES

No matter what you pay for plants, if they don't suit your particular needs, they are not a good investment. Even free plants require time and expense that you cannot afford to waste on disappointing specimens. But some plants require less coddling than others do and offer more in return.

Going Native

The plants best suited to your area are those nature put there. Check with your Cooperative Extension Service, and ask at local nurseries for ideas and sources. The trick to incorporating native plants is to adapt your idea of what a beautiful yard looks like to what nature has to offer.

A word of caution: Not only is it bad manners to lift plants from the wild, it is often illegal; even collecting seeds from some plants may be restricted. Check with your local Audubon Society or native-plant society to determine whether a plant is endangered.

Going native doesn't necessarily mean including only local plants in the landscape. Trace your finger along the latitudes (horizontal lines) of a globe and you'll see that the forty-fifth parallel intersects Oregon, Maine, France, and Mongolia, meaning growing conditions in at least parts of these regions will be similar. Plants from similar zones often grow equally well in one as in another. Alpine plants from Switzerland flourish in rock gardens in Minnesota and Oregon. Cacti from Arizona prosper in any hot, dry area. The idea is to use plants found in similar regions.

The Value of a Plant's Character

As mentioned before, only the plants that suit your taste, as well as your site, belong in your garden. But once you have decided your preferences for the more obvious qualities, consider some characteristics that will really save you money in the long run.

Disease Resistance

Two rosebushes are next to each other in a border garden. One is practically defoliated, with the remaining leaves covered in black blotches. The other has full leaves and boasts blooms to boot. What makes the difference? Some plants are just naturally more resistant to disease than others are, and we don't always know why. Perhaps the cuticle, the waxy coating, on the leaves of the healthy rose bush is thicker, less acidic, or tougher than that of the sick rose bush. Physical and chemical attributes account for much of the mystique of natural resistance.

We may not know exactly *why* some plants resist illness, but we know disease resistance exists. Unfortunately, resistance often varies with climate or locale. Still, resistant varieties help you save the money you would spend on fighting plant diseases or replacing lost plants. Look for varieties that are resistant to diseases that are particularly prevalent in your area. The chart starting on page 256 offers a sampling, but seed catalogs and garden centers update varieties annually.

Drought Resistance

Plants that evolved in arid places had to adapt in order to survive. Thin leaves, a glossy coating, fuzzy stems, and fleshy plant parts all help prevent water loss. Cacti are the classic example of drought resistance. But other plants also tolerate a lack of water. Remember that newly transplanted specimens usually will need to be kept moist until they adapt to their new surroundings.

MORE ▶

DIRT CHEAP

For longer-lived plants, choose disease-resistant varieties appropriate for your growing conditions. It's worth it to spend a little more up front for a plant that will live longer and present fewer problems. Don't assume that certified-disease-free plants or resistant varieties will never get sick. Just as you can keep susceptible plants healthy with proper care, disease-resistant plants can get sick if not maintained properly.

A Sampling of Drought-Tolerant Plants

Annuals

Ageratum
Cosmos
Marigold
Mexican
   sunflower
Morning glory
Ornamental
   pepper
Portulaca
Rose campion
Santolina
Statice
Vinca
Zinnia

Perennials/Bulbs

Artemisia
Baby's breath
Blackeyed susan
Columbine
Coreopsis
Crocus
Delphinium
Echinacea
Iris (nonbearded)
Lamb's ears
Lavender
Narcissus

Ornamental
   grasses
Perennial flax
Poppy mallow
Red valerian
Sage
Sedum
Sweet William
Tulip
Yarrow
Yucca

Trees/Shrubs

Cotoneaster
Flowering
   quince, red
Golden rain
   tree
Juniper
Locust
Oak
Pine
Walnut

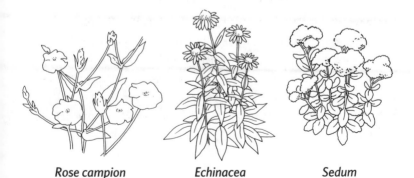

Rose campion   *Echinacea*   *Sedum*

Cold Hardiness

Gardeners in cold-climate areas rely on short-season, late-blooming, and cold-hardy plants. Plants that evolved in cold climates have developed some clever tricks for foiling frost. Short-season varieties take less time to flower or fruit than others of their type — they don't really tolerate cold; they avoid it. Late bloomers don't break bud in the spring until after hard frosts, hopefully.

A Sampling of Cold-Tolerant Plants

Perennials/Bulbs

Aster	Hosta
Bleeding heart	Iris
Columbine	Phlox
Coreopsis	Rudbeckia
Crocus	Sedum
Daylily	Tulip
Foxglove	Yarrow
Hardy geranium	Yellow corydalis

Trees/shrubs

Apple (most)	Plum (some)
Cotoneaster	Serviceberry
Juniper	Sour cherry
Kordesii and rugosa rose	Staghorn sumac
Late lilac	Weigela 'Minuet'
Norway spruce	
Pear	

Bleeding heart   *Columbine*   *Yarrow*

Low temperatures alone don't cause winter damage. Dehydrating winds, bright sun, and temperature fluctuations all contribute to damage. Water retained in cells, freezing and swelling and thawing and refreezing, causes structural damage to plants. Cells burst and irreparably damage tissues.

Cold-hardy perennials, shrubs, and trees have a unique method of surviving winter's chill called supercooling, by which they evacuate water from their cells prior to going dormant. If there is less water and less swelling, then less damage will occur. Decrease watering of perennials as the season progresses. This allows them to prepare for winter. Otherwise, you are wasting water at the expense of the plants themselves.

GREEN THUMB

DIRT CHEAP

This may sound a little obvious, but grow only what you and your family like to eat. No matter how abundant a crop you produce, it's waste of time and money if no one eats it.

Money-Saving Plant Varieties

Since many plants suitable for specific conditions have been discussed, let's consider those that perform well in a variety of garden settings. While there are bound to be exceptions, the plants listed in this section perform well all over the United States unless specifically noted. See Appendix B for an extensive list of vegetable varieties.

Choosing Garden Vegetables

An important consideration for a cost-effective plot is to grow only those crops that are cheaper to grow than buy. After all, why toil over a bed of spuds when you can buy 10 pounds for $3.59? Actually, there are a couple of sound exceptions to this rule. If your heart's desire is for a vegetable variety unavailable at the grocery store, grow your own. Another extremely important reason to bust your sod for spuds and other vegetables is pesticide use. Potatoes are among those vegetables grown with traditional mass-production methods that carry a high pesticide load.

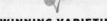
Buying Organic

Aside from your own backyard, organically grown food can be found from specialty shops to farmers' markets. Even most grocery stores nowadays have an organic section for fruits and vegetables. Certified organic produce is generally more expensive than chemically farmed food, but in some cases the cost difference is more justified than others. Broccoli, eggplant, cabbage, asparagus, avocados, onions, and frozen sweet corn and sweet peas are among the safest conventionally grown crops, so buying organic is not as critical. Same goes for bananas, pineapples, mangos, and kiwis.

It's healthiest to spring for the organic varieties of fruits and vegetables whose conventionally grown versions test high in pesticide load, including the following:

Apple	Lettuce	Potato
Celery	Nectarine	Spinach
Cherry	Peach	Strawberry
Grapes (imported)	Pear	Sweet bell pepper

DIRT CHEAP

The most cost-effective herbs you can grow, compared with buying them, are basil, borage, cilantro, lemon balm, oregano, pennyroyal, rosemary, sage, thyme, and tarragon. Other good choices include chamomile, chives, dill, mint, and parsley.

Herbs are among the most trouble-free plants to grow, rarely bothered by pests or diseases. This is an endearing quality to the gardener who likes to save time and money. Most are attractive plants that add beauty to the landscape, and many are exquisitely fragrant. They fit in anywhere; interplant into a border, or grow in containers, a window box, or a pot on a sunny kitchen windowsill.

GREEN THUMB

Common culinary herbs such as dill, oregano, sage, and tarragon suddenly become gourmet delights when picked fresh. Moreover, *all* herbs seem to taste better when you don't have to pay the high prices they bring at the market. Grow mints, chamomile, and lemon balm, among others, to create soothing teas at a fraction of the cost of store-bought. You can also dry herbs to use and enjoy all through the year or to give as gifts.

Ground Covers

Choices in ground covers have expanded wildly in the last few years. From play turf to low-maintenance juniper, there is something for every lifestyle and every pocketbook. As nice as a lawn is, when you consider the time and expense that goes into maintaining it, alternatives become all the more attractive. And most add visual interest that turf can't touch.

Best-Value Ground Cover Choices

Bellflowers
Boston ivy
Bugleweed
Chamomile*
Cotoneaster**
Creeping mahonia
Creeping phlox**
Crownvetch**
Dichondra*/***
English ivy

Gazania
Hen and chicks**
Irish moss
Juniper
New Zealand brass buttons
Ornamental brass buttons
Ornamental grasses (low-growing varieties)
Pachysandra
Portulaca**/***

Prostrate rosemary
Rockcress
Rock rose
Roses (low-growing and trailing varieties)
Sedum**
Silvervein creeper
Snow-in-summer
Strawberry

Sweet woodruff**
Thyme
Vinca
Virginia creeper
Wild ginger
Wintergreen
Zoysia***

*Tolerates foot traffic   **Drought tolerant once established   ***Not cold hardy

DIRT CHEAP

Many ground covers tolerate drought much better than a lawn can, which saves you money on watering, as well as mowing.

Landscape Shrubs

Shrubs and hedges can provide a contrast, focal point, or background for other plants in the yard or garden. They also provide a haven for birds. Standout varieties remain attractive even after their main growing season, and evergreens give year-round service.

Best-Value Landscape Shrubs

Arborvitae	Hollies	Oregon grape	Rose of Sharon
Blueberry	Hydrangea	Potentilla fructicosa*	Spirea
Cotoneaster*	Juniper*	Rhododendron	Viburnum
Forsythia	Lilac	Rose	

Drought tolerant once established

Growing Small Fruits

Though they are expensive in the supermarket, most small fruits are easy to grow and yield a good harvest. You can expect to pick a certain amount of fruit per plant, depending on the variety. Some examples are:

▶ Blackberry	12–25 pounds		▶ Elderberry	10–15 pounds
▶ Blueberry	4–5		▶ Gooseberry	8–10
▶ Currant	5–8		▶ Raspberry	2–4

For a detailed list of recommended high-productivity fruit varieties, see Appendix C.

CHAPTER 5

SAVE FROM THE START

When buying plants, seeds are much cheaper than transplants. For example, tomato seeds cost perhaps $3.25 for a packet of 20 seeds, or just over 16 cents each. The same variety sold as a seedling, however, might cost $3.25 for a single plant, 20 *times* more expensive.

Of course, you have to factor in the cost of growing the seed, but even expensive seed is still a bargain. Then there are the seeds you buy on sale or wholesale or those you save from your own plants. Outside of a few pennies for seed, soil, and water, the costs are negligible for a home-grown transplant. The important thing is to give your plants the right start in life so they'll thrive, giving you the best possible return for your dollar.

Seeds Have Needs

Tucked away in its cozy hiding place, protected by a tough seed coat, a baby plant waits to make its grand entrance into the world. When conditions of light, temperature, and moisture are just right, the embryo bursts forth. It carries just enough nutrition in the seed for the incredible feat of breaking free and stretching upward. Afterward, it makes its own food.

The main thing seeds need to start growing is to find a way to the soil, which is where you come in. Seeds may be direct seeded, which means planted directly into the garden where they will grow, or started in containers for later transplanting. Most plants are better suited to one method than the other.

Plants Suitable for Direct Seeding

Flowers		Vegetables	
Alyssum	Lupine	Beans	Okra
Calendula	Lychnis	Beet	Onion (sets)
California poppy	Marigold	Broccoli	Peas
Celosia	Morning glory	Cabbage	Potato (eye pieces)
Cornflower	Nasturtium	Carrot	Pumpkin
Cosmos	Portulaca	Cauliflower	Radish
Flax	Stock	Chard	Spinach
Forget-me-not	Sunflower	Corn	Squash
Godetia	Sweet William	Cucumber	Turnip
Larkspur	Zinnia	Lettuce	

Seed Germination Enhancement

When researchers put different seeds in a microwave oven, they did more than just make popcorn. They learned that a short burst of microwaves actually enhances germination by speeding up the metabolism of the seed.

It's another way to squeeze more from your seed budget, especially for older seed or for types with low germination rates. And since the best results were with small lots, it's perfect for home gardeners. One experimenter found that when low-germination-rate pepper seeds were exposed to 15 seconds in the microwave the germination rate improved by about 25 percent.

This method is best for small seeds, as it is easiest to get even exposure. Here's what to do:

▶ Place a thin layer in the center of a microwave oven, and heat for 10 to 30 seconds, depending on the size and moisture of the seed. The larger or drier the seeds, the more time it will take.

▶ Start at 10 to 15 seconds, and increase by 10 to 15 seconds on later batches if there is no improvement in germination rates.

▶ *Never microwave for more than about 30 seconds;* overheating kills the seed. In experiments sunflower seeds microwaved for 30 seconds germinated faster than those not microwaved, but those heated for 60 seconds didn't germinate at all.

Setting Your Seeds

Direct seeding is the original plan for seed-bearing plants. They flower and set seed, and some seeds manage to get a foothold. Prepare the seedbed by removing all weeds and cultivating the soil to break it into fine particles. Water the area the day before planting so the soil is moist.

You can broadcast seeds or plant them in rows. Spice dispensers make handy, free broadcasters. Scatter tiny seeds more evenly by mixing with fine sand as a carrying medium. To plant in rows use a dibble, made from a stick, a pencil, or your finger, to poke a hole the appropriate depth into the soil, and drop a seed or two in each hole. Use either method for raised beds or wide rows.

Once you've planted them, cover seeds lightly with fine soil. The standard rule of thumb is that seeds

GREEN THUMB

When starting vining plants, such as pole beans, scarlet runner beans, or sweet peas, plant a support system right along with them. Otherwise you risk killing or injuring young plants when you jab a stake through their roots later on.

should be covered with soil two or three times deeper than the seed's diameter. Gently press on the soil covering the seeds until the soil is firm. Watering is critical for seeds and seedlings; tender shoots will die if allowed to dry out.

MORE ▶

Dealing with Pests and Weeds

Once you've tilled your seedbed, you may wish to treat the soil with an organic pesticide such as diatomaceous earth, especially in soil freshly turned from sod. If soil-dwelling insects such as armyworms or cutworms get your plants before they emerge, you not only waste the money, time, and effort of planting, but you fall behind in the growing season.

Instead of using chemicals, however, you can save money by planning ahead. If you are preparing an established bed, till or cultivate as if for planting, but leave the bed empty for a couple of weeks to allow weed seeds to sprout. Then come back and pull or slice off the weeds with a scuffle hoe.

Another cheap trick, and much easier on your back, is covering the bed with clear plastic for 4 to 6 weeks to let the sun bake and kill off seeds, pathogens, and bugs alike. If you keep chickens, or you can borrow a few from a neighbor, pen them up in the garden for a week or so to till, debug, and fertilize for you (not to mention to provide you with eggs!).

Plant at the Right Temperature

It is important to know the temperature tolerance of the seeds you plant. Cool-season plants will sprout and grow at 40°F (4.4°C) due to the process of microbial breakdown; however, cold soil has few organic nutrients available to plants (see chapter 9 for ways to jumpstart plants in the cold). But warm-season plants will rot at 40°F. Most plants germinate very well at temperatures between 60 and 70°F (15.6 and 21.1°C).

Cool-Season Crops

Broccoli	Mustard	Peas
Carrot	Onion	Petunia
Chard	Pansy	Spinach
Lettuce		

Warm-Season Crops

Beans	Geranium	Peppers
Begonia	Marigold	Radish
Corn	Melon	Squash
Cucumber	Okra	Tomato

Dirt Cheap

Many gardeners prefer broadcast seeding, but I think it wastes seed. It *is* faster than placing each individual seed where it belongs. Much of the time saved is imaginary, though, because thinning the thickly sprouted seeds takes time as well.

Starting Seeds

You can start transplants either indoors in containers or outside in a cold frame (see page 228) to get a jump on the growing season. It's a good idea if you have a short growing season, and for plants such as tomatoes and peppers that originated in the tropics and require a long, warm growing.

Giving your plants an early start will allow them to begin producing earlier, giving you a much better return for your gardening investment. Always start in pots made of peat or other biodegradable material, and transplant them pot and all to avoid disturbing roots.

Plants Suitable for Starting in Containers

Flowers

Ageratum	Impatiens	
Anemone	Lobelia	
Aster	Lupine	
Astilbe	Nicotiana	
Begonia	Pansy	
Bleeding heart	Pelargonium	
Carnation	Petunia	
Columbine	Portulaca	
Coneflower	Potentilla	
Delphinium	Primrose	
Dusty miller	Salvia	
Gerbera daisy	Zinnia	
Godetia		

Vegetables

Broccoli
Brussels sprouts
Cabbage
Cantaloupe
Cauliflower
Eggplant
Lettuce
Peppers
Tomato

Seed-Starting Supplies

The only requirements for transplant containers is that they must be at least 2½ inches deep to allow for young, spreading roots, and they must have drainage holes. Those nicely matching plastic models at the garden center are a landfill nightmare. If you must buy them, use them carefully, wash thoroughly, and *reuse* them.

Cheap and Free Seed-Starting Kits

Looking for free containers to hold your seeds? The possibilities are endless! For starters, almost any food-safe container will do. Look around your house, garage, and workshop for other ideas.

▶ Cut milk cartons lengthwise and slice a few holes in the bottom for drainage.

▶ Large, wax-coated cereal boxes and Styrofoam take-out containers are made-to-order seed starters.

▶ For a built-in greenhouse effect, save clear plastic boxes from delis or bakeries. Poke holes in the bottom, fill, plant, and put the lid on.

▶ Wash out used margarine or yogurt cups and plastic trays from snack foods.

▶ Save toilet paper rolls, cut them in half widthwise, arrange on a tray, and fill.

▶ Piece together wooden flats from scrap lumber, but don't use old painted wood or treated lumber, as it may contain toxins that could leach into the container soil.

▶ Scrounge up trays to place beneath the draining containers. A shallow box lined with plastic wrap or a cookie tray will work in a pinch.

▶ Save plastic lids to put under larger pots.

Really Cheap Pots

You can recycle old newspapers to make made-to-order transplant pots for your indoor-grown seedlings. All it will cost you is a little time and inky fingers. The Paper Pot Maker or Paper Potter, which sells for around $14.00 in garden centers or through gardening catalogs or magazines, makes the task easy, but you can get essentially the same results using a drinking glass or tin can as a form. I find about 2½ inches around works great, but you can make the pots any size, based on the size of the form you use. You'll need:

▶ Newspapers, black-and-white print only; colored inks okay if you know they are soy-based

▶ A small jar, drinking glass, or tin can to serve as the form

▶ Tape to secure edges

MORE

How to make the pots:

1. Open a full sheet of newspaper, and fold in half so that the top is lined up with the bottom, then fold in half again. This should give you a strip about 3½ inches wide, 4 layers thick. (You can adjust the size of the finished pot by altering the number of folds.)

2. Place the strip against the jar so that an inch or so of paper extends past the end of it. This "extra" paper will be folded in to form the bottom of the pot.

3. Wrap the newspaper around the jar. Keep it fairly taut, but leave enough slack so that you can slide the jar out.

4. Tape the edge of the paper to itself to hold it together.

5. Fold the excess paper over to make the bottom of the pot. Tap the jar down onto the folded bottom to stamp it into shape, then tape the bottom to secure.

6. Slide the jar out, and fill your new paper pot with potting mix.

Be sure to keep the pots in a waterproof tray while seedlings are growing. At planting time you can unwind the paper from the roots, or put the seedling into the ground, paper pot and all.

Temperature is critical to how many seeds germinate and develop. Room temperature, 65 to 70°F (18.3 to 21.1°C), works well to germinate most plants, although some require higher or lower temperatures. Check seed packets, catalogs, or a good online source (see Resources) for specifics. Heating mats or tape underneath the seed containers encourage roots to grow downward. Once plants sprout, however, remove the bottom heat, as cooler temperatures produce sturdier plants.

GREEN THUMB

Sow the seed as for direct seeding. Don't worry about spacing. As soon as the seedlings show two to four leaves, carefully lift by the leaves and transplant into individual containers. Never pick up tiny seedlings by the stem because they can be crushed easily.

DIRT CHEAP

Know the individual light requirements of seeds you're germinating so you don't lose seedlings before they even sprout. A fluorescent light is a good investment, as it helps give your seedlings a strong, healthy start. You don't need a full-spectrum grow light for anything unless it has to flower and set fruit, so most seedlings do fine with just the cool range found in normal fluorescents.

Let There Be Light

Most seeds germinate best in darkness, but some won't sprout without a little light. Knowing the light requirements of the seeds you sow prevents mysterious disappointments. The light level is just as important after the seeds sprout. Seedlings need a balance of light and warmth to grow. Too much light and not enough heat and they may not grow at all. Start with lights on for 16 hours a day, no more than 12 inches above the seedlings, and gradually decrease to 12 hours.

Too much heat and not enough light causes them to grow pale and spindly. Plants grown on windowsills will do fine if the microclimate near the window is cool enough — just be sure to turn them regularly or they will bend toward the source of light.

The alternative is to purchase cool-watt fluorescent lights. Sold as shop lights in 4- and 8-foot lengths, the lights are inexpensive and perfectly adequate for seed starting. Hang them within a few inches of the plants' tops, and adjust the height of the lights as the seedlings grow.

Transplant for the Long Run

Whether homegrown or store-bought, transplants represent an investment in time or cash. They are usually easy to establish as they already have an active root system. Unfortunately, the stress of transplanting can cause plants to go into temporary shock. Reduce transplant shock by waiting until it is warm enough for the species and taking the time to harden them off before planting.

Be Tough: Hardening Off

Hardening off is a physical toughening of plant tissues. Whether you are bringing home plants from the garden center or preparing your homegrown transplants, it is a crucial step. Begin by placing the plants outside for about 30 minutes in a protected site, near a south wall, for instance. Even a gentle breeze can seem like a howling gale to tender young plants.

The next day increase the plants' time and exposure to the elements. How long will depend on the weather, but a good rule of thumb is to double the exposure daily. Bring them in early if the weather turns to blazing heat, a sudden hail storm or blasting wind. An exact schedule isn't required and the plants will pick up where they left off. Continue this routine for about a week.

MORE

Ready, Set, Plant!

Transplant on an overcast day or in the late afternoon. Use a garden trowel to dig holes for the transplants 1 to 2 inches deeper than the roots of the plants. Sprinkle a little fertilizer or 1 inch of compost at the bottom of each hole. Refill the hole so the transplant rests at the same depth it grew at in the container. Gently loosen the transplant's roots, and place it in the hole. Pat into place, and water.

Now Is Not the Time to Be Tough

Coddle the transplants for a few days even though they have been hardened off. They will suffer less shock and will grow more quickly. Water frequently, but don't drown them. If the weather is windy, create a windbreak by placing a board or bale of straw between them and the prevailing wind. And if it gets too hot or sunny, rig a shade cloth over them.

DIRT CHEAP

Most store-bought bedding plants aren't ready to move right from the greenhouse to the real world. Hardening off transplants takes only a few days and pays off in the long-term survival rate and vigor of your mature plants.

To further protect your investment, two-liter plastic bottles and gallon jugs make great individual cloches (hot-cap covers) for newly transplanted seedlings (see page 222).

Planting Perennials

You can transplant most perennials at any time, but spring and fall will give the best results. Top growth is slower at these times, yet roots are still developing. At this stage the plant has the greatest chance of establishing roots before going dormant for the winter.

1. Water the plant thoroughly several hours before you plan to transplant it.

2. Dig a hole about twice as big around as the roots of the plant and a few inches deeper. Loosen the soil at the bottom of the hole with a spading fork to encourage root growth downward. For bedding plants, you can sprinkle a little fertilizer or compost in the bottom and cover with soil.

3. Gently slide the plant from the container without breaking any roots. Carefully loosen some of the root soil (a fork is a good tool for this job). Tease any roots that have begun to grow in circles free of the root ball.

4. Place the plant in the hole to gauge the depth. Remove the plant, then dig a little deeper or refill the hole a little as necessary to adjust the planting depth to match the level it's been growing in the container.

MORE ▶

5. Once the plant sits at the proper depth, backfill with soil from the hole and water well. Pay a little extra attention until the roots are established.

Planting Vines and Climbers

Transplant vines or climbers from containers the same way as you do perennials. It is usually best to transplant in the spring to give the plant a chance to establish well in advance of winter.

Plant climbers that have been grafted to a rootstock, such as wisteria and climbing roses, with the graft union below the soil level. This protects the union from extreme temperatures and prompts the climber to send out its own roots.

GREEN THUMB

Prepare a perennial bed by tilling and amending the soil at least a few days before planting. Doing this the fall before you intend to plant is ideal, as it gives the soil plenty of time to settle and mellow.

Make sure you plant perennials at the proper depth. Transplant most perennials at the same level they grew at in the container or the field, usually with the crown at soil level. Plants that require dampness near the crown, such as Solomon's seal and hostas, should be planted a little lower than they were previously growing.

Clematis, whether grafted or on its own roots, develops more buds if set about 2 inches deeper than it originally grew.

Most climbers grown on their own roots, such as climbing hydrangea, grapes, and honeysuckle, should be set in the ground at about the same level they were growing in the container or *slightly* deeper. The Colorado State University Extension Service serves an area that certainly sees its fair share of cold winters, yet their motto when planting trees, shrubs, and vines is: "If you plant them high, they never die. If you plant them low, you never know."

MORE ▶

Never Amend Backfill

By digging a hole and filling it with amendments or foreign soil, you create an artificial environment with a dramatic interface between it and the surrounding native soil. In effect, you make an underground container. Because water does not flow freely between the two media, plant roots develop within the planting hole, much as they would in a container. They eventually circle and tangle around the edge of the hole.

At first, the plant will look normal; in fact, most plants will appear to thrive. After a while, however, the plant becomes virtually potbound and dies, leaving the conscientious backfiller to wonder why.

Planting climbers takes some planning, as you'll need to install a trellis or place the new plant near an existing support, such as a fence or tree. Supports, while necessary for climbers, pose a few challenges. For example, they can shelter the growing plant from essential rain or sprinkler water. If you use another plant as a support, the two will compete for water and nutrients.

Plant climbers at least a foot from the support to reduce water deflection and allow for adequate air circulation. But if using a tree as a vining support, plant the vine nearer the trunk, since competing feeder roots of the tree spread out near the dripline rather than near the trunk.

DIRT CHEAP

One of the fun parts about transplanting perennials is that once they are established, they are an endless source of free plants. Try arranging extensive borders using just the plants you propagate yourself (it's okay to sneak in a few store-bought plants if you can't resist).

CHAPTER 6

PLANT WELLNESS PAYS

Healthy plants are attractive and productive plants. They suffer less from pests and disease and resist stress from heat, cold, wind, and drought. They make the best possible use of available water and nutrients. In short, healthy plants give you the most for your money. It's worth taking care of them from the beginning.

How Fertilizers Work

Plants can only use nutrients that have been reduced to the molecular form. Chemical fertilizers work fast because they have already been processed into the molecular form, whereas organic fertilizers must first be broken down by soil microbes. Microbe activity depends on soil temperature. Below 70°F (21.1°C), soil microorganisms work slowly, which provides a slow, steady release of nutrients.

Chemical fertilizers dissolve fairly quickly, which is why the instructions say to water thoroughly after application. Unfortunately, this ready solubility also means that chemical fertilizers, unlike slow-release organics, leach more quickly from the soil.

Organic fertilizers are not necessarily more costly than synthetics. This is commonly misstated, because the measurable amount of nitrogen, phosphorus, and potassium in synthetic fertilizers costs less per pound than those in many commercially prepared organic fertilizers. But once you know, roughly, the fertilizer analysis of organic compounds, you can mix your own fertilizers that are balanced for your particular needs, at a fraction of the cost (see page 143 for details).

Organic or Synthetic?

A common misconception is that synthetic fertilizers are better than organic. Another misunderstanding is that organic is better than synthetic. You can make political or environmental arguments for synthetic or organic fertilizer, but the plants can't tell the difference as long as the proper nutrients are available. However, don't forget the many benefits of adding humus to your soil, which only organic amendments can supply.

Brand names mean nothing to plants. It's the fertilizer analysis that counts — the list of three, sometimes four, numbers noted on the bag. They stand for the percentage of nitrogen (designated by the international chemical symbol N), phosphorus (P), potassium (K), and, when present, sulfur (S) in the product, in that order.

As mentioned in chapter 1, these are the major elements plants need (except sulfur, which is a secondary element). Trace elements are also necessary, but manufacturers may or may not list them on labels. Organic fertilizers are much more likely to include these than chemical formulas are.

DIRT CHEAP

For the best results with the least expense, strategically combine fertilizers. In the spring, while the soil is still cool, apply chemical fertilizer to lawn, flower borders, and vegetable gardens. Once the soil is warm, work in compost or another low-cost organic source.

How Much Fertilizer?

The most common mistake gardeners make is thinking "more is better." If a bag of fertilizer says to apply a cup for every 10 feet of row, then 2 cups must make plants *really* grow, right? That is not the case. Manufacturers base their instructions on the ability of plant roots to absorb nutrients in a set amount of time. This rate varies with the type, age, and health of the plant, as well as the soil type and texture.

Most commercial fertilizers list application rates right on the bags. Follow these instructions, and don't be tempted to fall into the trap of thinking more is better. Since nitrogen is the element lost most quickly from the soil, manufacturers often figure rates based on a plant's need for this essential nutrient.

A fertilizer analysis of 4-8-6 means the product is 4 percent nitrogen. It takes 25 pounds of this product to yield 1 pound of actual nitrogen; 4 percent of 25 pounds is 1 pound. To determine the pounds of product it takes to yield 1 pound of nitrogen, use this formula:

Pounds of product needed = 1 ÷ percent of nitrogen in product

Now you need to find out how much nitrogen your garden needs. For a 1,000-square-foot garden, you need 1 pound of nitrogen. But what if your garden is 748 square feet? Here's the equation:

Pounds of product to supply 1 pound of nitrogen × the square feet of garden ÷ by 1,000 = pounds of product needed

For our example this figures as follows:

25 × 748 ÷ 1,000 = 25 × 0.748 = 18.7 pounds of product for your garden

Tailor-Made Fertilizer

Plant group	Beans Beet Carrot Corn Lettuce Radish Spinach Tomato	Cabbage Cauliflower Celery Kale Onion Parsley Peas Turnip	Cucumber Melon Pumpkin Rhubarb Roses Squash
N-P-K requirements	2-4-5	3-4-3	5-10-5
Blood meal (15-11.3-0.7)	0.7 pounds (0.3 kg)	1.6 pounds (0.7 kg)	1.2 pounds (0.5 kg)
Bone meal (4-21-0.2)	1 pound (0.5 kg)	2 pounds (0.9 kg)	2.4 pounds (1.1 kg)
Wood ashes (0-1-4.3)	8.3 pounds (3.8 kg)	6.8 pounds (3.1 kg)	6.4 pounds (2.9 kg)
Total pounds	10 (4.5 kg)	10	10

How to Fertilize Frugally

Fertilizers come in several forms, from quickly absorbed liquid solutions to slow-release powders and granules to compost, which breaks down even more gradually. Fertilizer spikes or compressed tablets do the measuring for you and simplify application as well, but as in all things, you pay extra for the convenience. Different types of fertilizers require different methods of application.

▶ **Sprinkle granules** around the base of plants, scratch into the soil, and water thoroughly to dissolve.

▶ **Shovel a layer of compost** or manure over the soil at the base of the plants, and scratch in with a hoe. This method is called sidedressing.

▶ **Apply liquid fertilizers** to either the soil or the leaves. This is called foliar feeding. Plants can absorb nutrients in solution through their leaves as well as their roots. In fact, they absorb them more quickly through the leaves. Apply these products with a sprayer or dissolve in a watering can and apply by hand.

For lawns a spreader broadcasts granular fertilizer evenly over the surface of the grass, or you can buy a liquid fertilizer applicator that attaches to your hose. Either one is a fair investment. You can also fertilize woody landscape plants by broadcasting the product throughout the lawn and just outside the dripline and watering it in.

If landscape plants are growing on the lawn, another option is to punch holes with a soil probe or soil auger attached to an electric drill, and put the fertilizer into the holes. This prevents burning the grass with an overdose of nitrogen. Make the holes 1 to 2 inches across and about 8 inches deep, spaced about 2 feet apart. Don't place them close to tree trunks, though, as the feeder roots are outwards, toward the dripline.

Tea Time

What can you do if you've got great compost, but your plants need a shot of nutrition right away? The answer is to brew up a batch of fabulous, free "tea." Nutrients from the compost leach into the water, which you then use to water your garden or to foliar feed. Here's how:

1. Scoop a couple of pounds of finished compost into a bag — use an old pillowcase, old pantyhose, a gunnysack, a flour sack, or any bag made of porous fabric.

2. Tie off the top and set in a 5-gallon bucket. Use larger containers and more compost if you need more fertilizer.

3. Fill the bucket with water (untreated or rainwater is best) to the top of the bag and let it sit for a day or two. The ideal temperature for "tea brewing" is around 70°F (21.1°C), but a range of 55 to 95°F (12.8 to 35°C) works.

Note: A lot of recipes recommend using an aerator as the tea is cooking in order to provide oxygen to the microbes in the water. In the absence of oxygen, anaerobic bacteria can flourish, leaving a tea that smells bad and contains more bad microorganisms than good ones.

The old-style method works well most of the time, but if you get stinky tea, don't spray it on your plants. Some recipes also recommend adding a tablespoon or two of horticultural molasses to boost the good/aerobic microorganisms.

Cut the Grass, Save the Green

Discourage weeds and boost your lawn's pest and disease resistance with the simple act of mowing your lawn properly. You'll save money on weed killer, fertilizers, and pesticides. Proper mowing means:

▶ **Mow to the right height.** Short-cropped lawns develop shallow roots and are susceptible to drought, root-feeding insects, and diseases. They also allow more weeds to germinate. Bluegrass and fine fescues thrive best mowed to 2 to 3 inches tall.

▶ **Mow on a regular schedule.** The standard wisdom is to never cut more than one-third of the blade at once, so time mowings to your lawn's growth. Cutting too close stresses the grass.

▶ **Mow with a sharp blade.** Dull blades tear and damage grass, creating entry points for diseases such as leaf spot.

Save the Most — Compost!

Composting is one of the many small miracles that take place in our gardens. It is the process by which weeds, garden debris, and other organic matter break down into dark, rich, crumbly soil, turning trash into treasure. The process occurs naturally without our help, but we can encourage it by controlling the circumstances under which it happens.

Straw into Gold

What makes compost so great? It is rich in nutrients derived from plant and animal matter. Unlike many store-bought soil amendments, it also contains trace elements. And the process of composting helps purify the end product by killing many seeds and harmful organisms present in the raw ingredients. The key is heat — though piles can heat up even hotter, compost is finished when it has reached a minimum of 135°F (57.2°C) for several days. It's the closest thing gardeners have to spinning straw (and weeds and manure and eggshells and more!) into gold.

Great! Where Do I Get Some?

The good news is that anybody can make compost. Actually, compost will make itself without any help from you at all! All organic matter rots eventually, but you can speed up the process by combining different types of matter, ventilating or turning the mix to add oxygen, and keeping it moist.

Compost Needs Nitrogen and Carbon

In terms of composting, organic matter pretty much divides into either nitrogen-based material or carbon-based material. Microbes burn approximately 1 part of nitrogen for every 25 parts of carbon they digest. So you need at least 1 part of nitrogen-based material for every 25 parts of carbon-based material in your compost pile. More nitrogen material is fine if you have it. Materials high in nitrogen, such as alfalfa meal, blood meal, and urea, act as pile activators by jump-starting the microbes' process.

Which materials are nitrogen based, and which are carbon? In general materials higher in nitrogen are green (grass clippings, weeds, kitchen waste) and those higher in carbon are brown (straw, leaves, sawdust). Other ingredients add phosphorus, potassium, and trace minerals. Eggshells, wood ashes, banana skins, melon rinds, orange peels, stale bread, apple peels, potato skins, pea pods, and tea leaves are great for composting.

Nitrogen-based Green

Alfalfa	Green weeds	Seaweed
Coffee grounds	Manures	Stalks, stems, and leaves from crops
Grass clippings	Milfoil (lake weeds)	

Carbon-based Brown

Cocoa hulls	Dry leaves	Sawdust
Hay	Peanut hulls	Straw
Last year's mulch	Peat moss	

Good Compost, Bad Compost

The list of things that can go into the compost pile is long and varied. In addition to those materials listed below and in the box on page 149, you can put nearly anything that grows in a compost pile, including most of your kitchen waste.

There are a few things, however, that *do not* belong in your compost pile. Also, it's critical to know your sources of material. Unwittingly introducing toxins to your garden is at best a money-losing proposition. Do not put the following in your pile:

You can add many items whole to the compost pile, and they will degrade just fine. But larger items, such as cornstalks, hedge trimmings, and spent broccoli plants, will break down much more quickly if chopped into smaller pieces first. Cutting up large pieces into smaller ones creates more surface area on which the microbes can work. Reduce large pieces by running over a shallow pile of them with a lawn mower, hacking them up with an ax, or throwing them in a chipper/shredder.

▶ Weeds that have gone to seed; the seeds may survive

▶ Obviously diseased or insect-infested material that can infect your plants

▶ Meat, grease, or fat; it stinks and attracts vermin

▶ Pig, cat, or dog feces, which may transfer parasites to the garden

▶ Grass clippings or weeds that have been treated with long-lasting weed killers

▶ Manure or bedding from animals fed on pasture treated with long-lasting herbicides

▶ Poison oak, ivy, or sumac; these plants contain urushiol, an oil that sparks rashes and allergic reactions, and composting can spread it through the garden

▶ Pine needles or large branches; they don't harm the pile but take years to decompose

DIRT CHEAP

Alfalfa is a great way to activate a compost pile, and it costs pennies. Toss in handfuls from bales (old or rained-on bales are cheap or free), or use an alfalfa-meal product. Horse feed, rabbit-food pellets, and even some brands of cat litter are almost pure alfalfa meal.

Ready, Set, Compost!

You can make compost as easily and cheaply as any leaf-dropping tree does. All you need are the ingredients and as much time as you are willing to devote to the project.

The dimensions of the pile affect how quickly it breaks down. The pile must be at least 3 feet high by 3 feet across in order to have enough mass to retain the heat generated in composting. As the microbes work, temperatures can reach 140°F (60°C) inside the pile. These high temperatures kill many weed seeds and most disease organisms.

Piles about 4 feet by 4 feet will work fine, but piles much larger than 5 feet around take a lot of watering and turning to keep moisture and oxygen supplied to those busy microbes.

Chemical-Free Compost

Although composting breaks down most chemicals available to homeowners (that is, people without a special license to purchase highly toxic chemicals) into harmless substances, trimmings from other sources (golf courses, professional landscapers, commercial farms) may have been treated with chemicals that can persist and poison the garden.

Beware of material treated with clopyralid, sold as Confront. It does not break down during composting. Don't use bedding or manure from animals that have grazed on pasture treated with hormone-based aminopyralid, sold as Forefront. It deforms bean, potato, and tomato plants, decreasing or eliminating yields.

You Don't Need a Fancy Bin

For the sake of appearances, or ease of handling, you may wish to enclose your compost pile in some fashion, rather than just piling it up on the ground. You can purchase many sizes and styles of heavy-duty plastic bins, but my favorite material for this job is a 10- to 12½-foot length of 48-inch-wide hardware cloth, ½- × 1-inch mesh. It is sturdy enough to be freestanding, forms a circle of perfect dimensions for composting, and won't leak any small pieces of the pile.

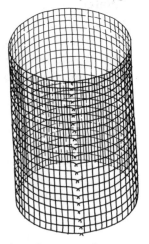

Lumber scraps and chicken wire, salvaged concrete blocks, or bales of straw arranged together will also serve the purpose. Don't use pressure-treated wood, however, as chemicals can leach into the compost and be absorbed later by your plants.

A wire compost bin is cheap, easy to use, lasts forever, and stores almost anywhere. Bend over a few of the loose wires on one edge to form hooks to attach it to the other edge to form a cylinder.

If You Build It, Stuff Will Rot

While there are no hard-and-fast rules for building a compost pile, you should follow a few basic rules.

▶ **Layer.** You can start out by layering nitrogen materials and carbon materials with a bit of soil, but the first time you turn the pile this neat arrangement is shot. The most convenient way to compost is to toss in whatever is available at the moment.

▶ **Water.** An occasional sprinkling with the garden hose provides the microbes with water they need to survive. Don't let piles get dripping wet, however, as precious plant nutrients will leach out and aerobic microbes will drown. Cover your pile during rainy weather or if it is within sprinkler range.

▶ **Turn.** Turning the pile provides aerobic conditions for you and the pile — you get the exercise, and the pile gets a fresh supply of oxygen for those hard-working microbes. If you are using a bin, disassemble it, grab a fork, and start working. Turn the outsides of the old pile into the center of the new one so they will be exposed to microbial action. Sprinkle the pile with water intermittently as you turn it. The more frequently you turn the pile, the more quickly the compost will decompose.

Preventing Pests and Disease

Many pesticide labels advise spraying at the first sign of a problem, which is good advice. Early, consistent spray schedules help control pests and diseases. It's even better and cheaper, however, to prevent bugs and plant diseases in the first place.

A Healthy Environment Pays Off

Healthy plants are less susceptible to physical stress, disease, or pests. In fact, studies show insects recognize and target ailing plants. The best way to manage your garden is to keep a watchful eye on plants. Take time to notice indications that a plant may be susceptible to damage.

▶ Watch for puddling around the plants after rain — poor drainage can suffocate roots.

▶ Look for unusual growth patterns, spots on leaves or stems, curling leaves, or other oddities.

▶ Make sure plants are not overcrowded; damp, stagnant air trapped near foliage often leads to disease.

Weed Out the Competition

The first line of defense is to kick the competition when it's down. Don't allow weeds to get a foothold. They rob the soil of the water and nutrients that you put there for cultivated plants. They can harbor diseases or serve as alternate hosts for pests. If allowed to grow, they may shade plants from sunlight, block air circulation around foliage, or crowd out crops entirely.

Methods of Attack

Rather than battle established weeds and the problems they create, get them before they get you. If you start early in the season and make it a habit to do a little weed control every few days, you will avoid a massive, backbreaking chore later in the summer. Here are some ways to jump-start the process:

▶ **Spray a preemergent herbicide,** which kills weeds *before* they emerge. Corn gluten is being tested as a safe alternative to chemical-based preemergent herbicides. It only kills the roots of sprouting seeds so is safe to use around established plants; in addition, it is 10 percent nitrogen, so it makes a good early-spring fertilizer.

▶ **Lay down a heavy, water-permeable fabric** between landscape plants, then cover with soil or decorative mulch. It blocks light and physically blocks weeds from sprouting. This is not the cheapest option, but the time and money you save over other forms of fighting weeds may make it a good choice. Putting down a thick layer of mulch is a similar tactic.

▶ **Scrape away young weeds** with a hoe, making sure to cultivate carefully around tender garden plants to avoid damaging roots. Use a scuffle hoe or toothed-wheeled weeder to tear out weeds while they are still small.

▶ **When all else fails,** get down on your knees and yank up weeds by their roots. It's good exercise, and a well-weeded patch leaves any gardener with a real sense of accomplishment.

DIRT CHEAP

Keep a watchful eye out for signs of insect pests or disease so you can take steps to control the damage early. Keep in mind, however, that unless they are causing actual damage, you may not need to take any action.

Ban Bugs with the Barrier Method

One of the best methods to prevent insect damage is to physically prevent bugs from touching plants in the first place. The following methods are very effective and reasonably inexpensive when done properly.

DIRT CHEAP

Treat fabric covers with respect to get your money's worth. Once the integrity of the fabric is breached, a single grasshopper can expand the hole so it's large enough to allow in a horde.

▶ Work cautiously around them, as a careless swing of the hoe will tear the fabric.

▶ Never walk on them; always go around.

▶ Don't drive stakes through them as anchors. Fabric anchored by stakes will not always keep bugs away, and the stakes will cause rips.

▶ Cut the fabric down to a size you can handle easily.

▶ Above all else, fold or roll up fabric covers at the end of the season, and store them properly. Don't just drop them in a pile on the floor of the garden shed, since mice find them irresistible for winter housing.

Row Covers

These are sheets of spun-bonded polyester that can be draped over food crops to eliminate insect problems. They are light-weight enough to drop directly onto most crops, or you can create a frame for the covering with PVC pipe, bamboo stakes, or scrap lumber. The fabric allows most available sunlight and water to pass through freely yet protects plants against wind, hail, slight frost, and windborne weed seeds, as well as bugs, birds, and small animals.

It is critical to cover crops early, before bugs get to them. For plants that tend to get buggy, such as broccoli or spinach, planting or transplanting time is the best time to cover them. A sprinkling of inexpensive diatomaceous earth raked into the soil will kill any current soil-dwelling inhabitants so that you don't wind up sealing bugs *in* with the transplants, beneath the covers. This is especially important for direct-seeded melons, a special favorite of soil-dwelling cutworms.

GREEN THUMB

Leave enough slack in the fabric to allow for the eventual growth of the plants, and anchor the fabric along the edges with dirt, rocks, pipe, or planks. Thorough anchoring is very important. It prevents the fabric from blowing off and seals off small spaces that hungry bugs can squeeze into. Lift the cover occasionally to monitor a plant's progress, and adjust the covering to allow for plant growth.

Covers are most convenient for plants that don't have to flower in order to produce a harvest, such as carrots or broccoli. Covers will work for plants that flower, such as cucumbers, as long as you remove the covers in time for pollination to occur or practice hand pollination.

Stem Collars

Stem collars protect tender transplants from cutworms, underground caterpillar-like bugs that will devastate beans, broccoli, cantaloupe, and a vast array of other plants with equal zeal. They are especially prevalent in new gardens freshly dug from sod or in weedy gardens. A dash of diatomaceous earth will eliminate cutworms that are present at application.

But for continuing, not to mention organic, protection, use stem collars. Stiff paper or cardboard is often recommended for collar making, but one of the best and cheapest

DiRT CHEAP

Sometimes pest control is not as cost-effective as a do-it-yourself project. For example, gardeners lucky enough to have large shade trees, but unlucky enough for those trees to become infested or diseased, should consult a professional. The problem with trying to spray a large tree yourself is that its sheer size often makes for an ineffective application. Without proper equipment you simply cannot get adequate coverage, and without adequate coverage you are wasting your money, not to mention risking harm to yourself. Always check professionals' credentials, and ask for references.

substitutes I have found is a simple plastic drinking straw. Cut into 1½-inch-long pieces. Slit the pieces up one side, pull the plastic apart, and fit it around the stem of each transplant. Gently push the plastic down beneath soil level, about ¼ inch, or just far enough to hold it in place, being very careful not to dig into the tender roots, and you have a plastic barrier no cutworm can chomp or climb.

Chemical Warfare

Sometimes a barrier isn't the answer. You wouldn't want to drape a cover over a rosebush or shimmy up an apple tree with a bolt of cheesecloth. In situations such as these you may prefer to spray a pesticide. How do you tell if you need to spray? Good advice to any gardener is to make sure there is actual damage before embarking on a control program. Many insects cohabit peacefully with your plot and never damage anything.

Choosing Conventional Chemicals

What you spray depends on several factors, one of which is your budget. Chemical pesticides are expensive in more ways than one. Research has determined that toxins, once commonly used in the garden, can cause a range of ills from birth defects to cancers. Accidental ingestion by pets and children occurs every year, with tragic results. Toxins also wipe out beneficial insects, such as bees and ladybugs. And misapplication of chemical pesticides often results in plant damage.

MORE ▶

As with chemical fertilizers, the biggest problem home gardeners have with pesticides is over application. Always follow label instructions to the letter. These are not mere recommendations, they are the law — it is illegal to misuse pesticides.

Each product lists what insects it is effective against and on which plants it is safe to use. A general pesticide with a wide range of applications, such as acephate, will handle most problems of home gardeners.

Opting for Organic

Organic pesticides, such as botanically derived rotenone, pyrethrum, and sabadilla, are good substitutes for chemical products. They pose less threat of environmental damage because they break down quickly, without leaving long-term residues. Like their chemical counterparts, however, many organic pesticides also kill indiscriminately, wiping out pests and beneficial organisms alike.

Horticultural oils, which range from heavy, dormant oil sprays to the newer, lighter, refined sprays, smother insect pests where they sit. They knock out small twig- and leaf-clinging bugs like aphids, leaf miners, caterpillars, mealy bugs, and beetles. Follow product directions, as some are meant to be sprayed only when plants are dormant, while others can be used throughout the growing season.

Looking at Alternatives

Some of the most promising pest-control products are ones that cause disease — generating pest-specific disease organisms that spring to life like sea monkeys when mixed with water. They only harm the bug for which they are intended. Some examples include several forms of the bacteria *Bacillus thuringiensis* (Bt), marketed under various brand names and effective at battling caterpillars and Colorado potato beetles; *Nosema locustae*, a grasshopper disease that prevents successive generations from hatching; and *Bacillus popilliae*, or milky spore disease, which wipes out Japanese beetle grubs.

DIRT CHEAP

Some of the best methods of insect control are free. Hand-picking insects, a fun hobby in its own right, is quite effective at controlling populations of larger insects such as tomato hornworms, Colorado potato beetles, and cucumber beetles. Pop the bugs into a bucket of soapy water to finish them off. When you're sure the bugs are dead, pour out into a storm drain, down the toilet or just away from your house and garden; they'll decompose naturally. While you're picking mature bugs, pick or squash any pest larvae or eggs you find, too.

Homemade Insect Controls

Commercial pesticides, whether conventional or organic, can be expensive, and they are not always necessary. You can make effective substitutes for a spray at home very inexpensively. Do a spot check on ornamentals prior to all-out spraying to test for sensitivity, and always be sure to coat all areas of the plant, including the undersides of leaves. Try some of the following time-tested recipes on your garden:

Soap Spray

Soap is one of the best combatants against aphids and other soft-bodied pests. Mix about 3 tablespoons of a mild laundry soap, such as Ivory Snow or an organic formula (not laundry detergent — soaps and detergents are different substances), or a tablespoon of dishwashing liquid (again, look for organic formulas; they break down quickly without harming the environment) with a gallon of water and spray on both sides of leaves.

The spray only works by actually contacting the bugs; there is no residual pesticide effect. Some plants, such as cole crops and certain ornamentals, can suffer from phytotoxicity, or burning of foliage, from soaps, so it's a good idea to test a small area first, before applying wholesale. Repeat applications can intensify plant sensitivity.

Tobacco Tea

To make this effective homemade brew, you'll need a cup of tobacco leaves, from collected cigarette butts or broken cigarettes. Place in a cloth bag, and steep in a gallon of water for an hour up to a few days. Add ¼ teaspoon of soap to act as a surfactant. This spray is highly effective against aphids, thrips, and leafhoppers, a testimony to the toxicity of nicotine.

Caution: Don't spray on or near tomatoes, eggplants, or peppers. Tobacco can carry tobacco mosaic virus, which is deadly to nightshade family crops. It's rare because most tobacco varieties grown today are resistant, but why take the chance? For the same reason, after spraying, wash thoroughly before working around these plants.

Tomato Leaf Tea

Tomato-leaf tea works in two ways. The first is through toxic alkaloid compounds in the leaves (likewise in potato and tobacco leaves) that kill aphids and corn earworms (also known as tomato fruit worm). The second is by attracting trichogramma wasps, which come for the spray but stay to parasitize earworm eggs.

Make tomato-leaf tea by soaking 1 or 2 cups of chopped leaves overnight in 2 cups of water, strain through cheesecloth, then dilute with 2 more cups of water. When spraying, be sure to cover the undersides of leaves and growing tips, as this is where aphids congregate. The spray is not a contact poison to people and pets, but it can cause allergic reactions. Don't ingest, and be sure to wash away any leftovers.

MORE

Herb Sprays

Herb sprays have been around for years, and multiple studies confirm their effectiveness. Sage and thyme oil and alcohol extracts of hyssop, rosemary, sage, and thyme reduce damage to cabbage by caterpillars. Tansy spray repels cabbageworm; wormwood and nasturtium teas repel aphids from fruit trees. Other herbs, including catnip, chive, feverfew, marigold, and rue deter leaf-feeding pests.

Since herb sprays are rather a custom process, feel free to experiment, but the general process is to chop up or process in a blender 1 or 2 cups of fresh herb leaves with 2 cups of water; let soak overnight, strain, add ¼ teaspoon of soap to help the spray stick, dilute with 2 more cups of water, and spray at will. Or take the easy way out: purchase essential oils and dilute them, a few drops of oil to a cup of water, increasing the amount of oil if necessary to see results.

Alcohol Spray

A spritz of alcohol wipes out mealybugs and scale. You can mix a cup of alcohol to a quart of water and spray, but a cheaper alternative is to paint straight alcohol directly on the icky critters using a cotton swab or small paintbrush.

DIRT CHEAP

Vinegar is a quick and inexpensive way to deter ants and kill slugs if sprayed on the soil around affected plants. Be careful, though, as it's also an effective spot herbicide — a 5 percent solution, which is what is generally sold in stores, kills weeds and grass and just about anything else green.

Garlic Spray

Garlic repels aphids, mealybugs, mites, cabbage loopers, grasshoppers, leafhoppers, squash bugs. It inhibits fungi and even helps deter deer and mice. Add garlic to any other spray for a boost, or combine 3 or 4 ounces of minced garlic with 1 or 2 ounces of mineral oil and let soak for at least 24 hours, add an ounce of soap then, strain and dilute 2 tablespoons of mix in a pint of water to spray. (Don't spray over 80°F.) Make oil-free spray by pouring just enough boiling water over a few chopped cloves to cover and steeping overnight. Strain and spray when cooled. Store in a cool, dark place and use within a week.

Chili Pepper Powders and Sprays

Any plant that contains capsaicin, such as chili peppers, black peppercorns, dill, ginger, and paprika, repels bugs. Dust the powder around the base of plants to repel ants (which are notorious aphid enablers), and dust on cabbage family plants, onions, and carrots to deter other bugs. This only makes sense from a cost perspective if you grow your own hot peppers, dry them, and pulverize into powder.

A spray that combines capsaicin with the sulfur compounds found in garlic is highly effective against many types of insects, including, unfortunately, many adult moths and butterflies. Combine 2 or 3 ounces of cayenne or other hot peppers, a similar amount of garlic, and a teaspoon of dishwashing liquid. (At least one recipe recommends soaking the cayenne or hot peppers in a couple teaspoons of mineral oil for 24 hours before processing.) Add 2 cups of water, and

MORE

puree in a blender. Strain and store in a glass jar. To use, dilute with water at the rate of 1 or 2 tablespoons per 2 cups water.

Boric Acid Powder

Borax (boric acid) is a cheap solution to infestations of cockroaches, ants, fleas, and some types of beetles. Sprinkle the powder where pests are a problem. It takes a few days to work, but bugs eventually die from desiccation. Caution: Though borax is generally safe to use as a pesticide, some animal studies suggest side effects, so just in case, minimize contact.

And Finally, Bug Spray

Using the enemy against itself is a favorite tactic of some organic gardeners. Collect a quantity of the offending bugs, and liquefy them in an old blender, reserved for this purpose. Strain, dilute with water (how much depends on how much area you want to cover and how many bugs you collected), and spray.

Natural, but Nasty Nonetheless

Pyrethrin is a botanical insecticide you can make if you grow the daisylike flower *Chrysanthemum cinerariifolium.* This spray packs a potent poison. Pour boiling water over the petals, and spray as soon as the concoction cools.

Caution: Keep your pets, especially cats, away from areas that have been sprayed. Pyrethrins are used in many flea and tick preventives, and overexposure can be harmful to animals. It is also toxic to fish, so don't spray where residue could drift into a natural waterway or garden pond.

The Good Guys

The use of beneficial organisms in the home garden is hardly new. If you think of Adam and Eve as the original garden pests, look at the effectiveness of one snake. Actually, snakes are wonderful, free rodenticides. They patrol for ground-level mice, shrews, bugs, and slugs. In return they need an accessible water source, maybe a nice, flat rock on which to sun themselves, and to not be run over by a lawnmower.

Bats are a fine addition to any garden. They consume many times their own weight of flying insects over the course of the gardening season. Persuade them to roost near your garden by putting up a little bat house — or even a condo complex.

Birds are valuable bug eaters. They will reward your thoughtfulness with years of dedicated service. Provide them with a birdbath, some cover in the form of bushes or trees, a small house or two, and perhaps a free meal every now and then.

Toads are underappreciated assets in the garden; they guzzle bugs daily. Encourage their presence with a damp, shady spot for them to hide in during hot, dry weather. A board propped up over a puddle is toad heaven.

Predatory and parasitic insects prey on other bugs for free, and unless you live in a vacuum, they usually come with the garden. Be careful not to annihilate them with broad-spectrum chemical pesticides.

Bugs Battling Bugs

Many insects, from barely visible mites to 6-inch-tall praying mantises, can be enlisted to work in your garden. You can purchase them, but your money would be better spent encouraging existing native populations. The trouble with many store-bought bugs is that they are disloyal and will probably leave.

Plant flowering herbs, such as thymes, mints, rosemary, sage, and dill for beneficial adult insects to eat. Or entice them by interplanting your crops with daisies, petunias, cosmos, nasturtiums, marigolds, and sunflowers. Provide a water source. The lingering dew on plant leaves is often sufficient; the constant moisture provided by drip irrigation is ideal. Most important, don't spray pesticides. Welcome the beneficials that occur naturally in your garden.

Common Beneficial Insects and Their Prey

Insect	Active Form	Prey
Ambush bug	Adult	Various
Assassin bug	Adult	Various
Big-eyed bug	Adult	Various
Encarsia formosa	Larvae and adult	Whitefly

Insect	Active Form	Prey
Green lacewing	Larva	Aphids, mealybugs
Ground beetles	Adult	Soil dwellers
Ladybug	Larva and adult	Aphids
*Nosema locustae**	Spores	Grasshopper
Parasitic wasps	Larvae and adult	Colorado potato beetle, tomato hornworm
Pirate bug	Adult	Various
Praying mantis	Nymph and adult	Caterpillars
Predatory mite*	Adult	Spider mite and whitefly
Soldier bug	Adult	Various
Spiders*	Juveniles, adults	Various
Tachinid fly	Larvae, adults	Caterpillars

*Not insects, but still useful pest-control organisms

Birds Are Great, but...

For the most part birds are very beneficial to the garden. They are wonderful insect predators, especially in the spring, when they need a supply of protein to feed their young. But hungry birds also can take a toll on freshly sown seeds, tender seedlings, and luscious fruits and berries. You may need one or more of the following controls.

Netting the Berry Patch

Netting is an important barrier to birds and some small animals. It is an absolute necessity with expensive berry crops, such as blueberries and strawberries. To keep greedy beaks away from berries, support netting on a framework several inches from the plants. Peeled poles or scrap lumber make inexpensive, rustic-looking frames. Handled carefully, netting will last indefinitely. Just be sure to check beneath the nets daily. Birds occasionally find ways to get stuck or tangled in nets.

Spun-bonded polyester row covers, placed over strawberry plants after they flower, is a good alternative. It not only keeps birds out while insuring they won't get tangled, it also bars yellowjackets and other bugs that mine the strawberries, leaving you with pitted hulls where sweet, juicy fruit should be.

MORE ▶

Covering Individual Plants

Pantyhose, cheesecloth, salvaged window screening, and other low-cost finds can create handy bird deterrents. Fasten any of these to a wire tomato cage for an individual plant protector.

A Defensive Line

Wire or fishing line, stretched between row markers over newly planted seeds, makes an inexpensive bird repellent. As birds approach for a landing, they are surprised by the unseen lines and quickly retreat to safer ground.

DIRT CHEAP

Scarecrows are cute but ineffective. By all means have fun building one from stuff you find around the house and garage, but don't spend a cent buying one.

Keeping Larger Critters Out

The most effective way to keep wayward wildlife from your garden is to construct a barrier. Fencing materials are certainly not cheap, but a well-constructed fence will serve for years. Woven wire, poultry netting, or welded wire will keep out most neighborhood pets and pests. The bottom of the wire should be buried below soil level if rabbits are a problem.

Foil persistent gophers and other ground-tunneling critters by lining the bottom and sides of raised planting beds with half-inch mesh hardware cloth (they'll chew right through flimsy wire mesh) before filling with soil, or by planting vulnerable veggies in a metal livestock watering tank. (Be sure to poke extra drainage holes in the bottom of the tank first.)

There are many options for deer fencing, but it needs to be 8 feet high to prevent them from jumping over. Leave approximately the top 18 inches of the wire unattached to any support. This wobbly fence discourages such climbing critters as woodchucks, raccoons, porcupines, and opossums. An alternative is to put up two rows of fencing to 6 feet tall, 6 to 8 feet

MORE ▶

apart, all around the garden to create a sort of above-ground dry moat. Use the fenced-in area as a dog run, chicken yard, llama pen, or other animal enclosure to get double your money from those materials.

Be Repulsive — DIY Deterrents

In lieu of expensive fencing, you may first want to try some of the many intriguing animal repellents available. Forget the store-bought solutions, and whip up your own thrifty alternatives. Here are a few suggestions:

▶ **Hair clippings** from the local barbershop or dog groomer scattered around the garden scare off critters that fear the ominous odor of humans or dogs. A few articles of really smelly dirty laundry, left about the garden at night, will also deter many wild animals, including deer, raccoons, and rabbits.

▶ **A sulfurous odor** can be created by letting a swill of raw eggs set until pungent. Sprayed around the garden, the strong scent repels deer by overwhelming their sense of smell and undermining their sense of security. The aroma fades quickly to human sensibilities but remains strong enough to be detected by more sensitive deer noses until washed away by rain or heavy sprinkling. Be sure to reapply afterward.

▶ **Dried blood meal** scattered around plants deters deer, ground squirrels, rabbits, raccoons, and woodchucks.

▶ **Ammonia.** Ironically, the nasty smell of rags soaked in ammonia repels skunks and rats.

▶ **Hot peppers, garlic, vinegar,** and water mixed with a squirt of dish soap and puréed in a blender discourages large nibblers, as well as insect pests, from taking a second bite from any garden fare on which it has been sprayed.

▶ **Vinegar** sprayed around the garden or soaked into rags and left at favorite spots will keep cats and rabbits from frequenting your garden beds.

▶ **Beer.** Set out a shallow tray of beer to lure and drown slugs. Of course, you should use cheap beer.

Repulsive Plants

Humans won't mind most of the following plants in the garden, but various animals and insects will steer clear if you plant them in and among your flowers and veggies. For instance, strongly scented plants, such as yarrow, wormwood, oregano, rosemary, lavender, and mints discourage deer that must rely on their sense of smell for protection.

Plant This	To Discourage These
Castor oil plant (highly toxic)	Gophers, moles
Garden rue	Cats
Garlic, onions, ornamental alliums	Woodchucks
Gopher spurge (*Euphorbia lathyrus*)	Gophers, moles
Wormwood	A wide range of mammals

Many plants work to ward off pesky insects as well.

Plant This	To Discourage These
Aster	Many insects
Basil	Flies, mosquitoes, asparagus beetles
Borage	Tomato worms
Calendula	Asparagus beetles, tomato worms
Catnip	Ants, aphids, flea beetles, Japanese beetles
Chives	Aphids, Japanese beetles, mites, whiteflies
Chrysanthemum	Japanese beetles, Mexican bean beetles
Coreopsis	Many insects
Coriander	Aphids, carrot flies, Colorado potato beetle, mites, and others
Garlic	Aphids, borers, Japanese beetles, spider mites
Geranium	Cabbage worms
Henbit	Just about any kind of bug
Horseradish	Potato beetles
Hyssop	Cabbage moths
Lavender	Moths
Marigold	Harmful nematodes, Mexican bean beetles

Plant This	To Discourage These
Marjoram	Many insects
Mints	Ants, aphids, cabbage moths, fleas
Nasturtium	Squash bugs and other beetles
Oregano	Cabbage butterflies, cucumber beetles
Parsley	Beetles in general
Radish	Cucumber beetles
Rosemary	Bean beetles, cabbage moths, carrot flies
Rue	Flies, Japanese beetles
Sage	Bean beetles, cabbage moths, carrot flies, slugs
Sunflower	Aphids
Tansy	Ants, fleas, flies, Japanese beetles, moths, striped cucumber beetles, squash bugs
Thyme	Cabbage worms

Discourage Plant Diseases

The first line of defense against plant diseases is good, overall plant health. This comes from proper weeding, feeding, watering, pruning, and choosing naturally disease-resistant varieties. It's always best to prevent than to have to treat. Here are a couple of cheap kitchen ingredients that can help keep plants healthy.

Baking Soda

Baking soda spray helps prevent powdery mildew on susceptible plants, such as beans, cucumbers, grapes, fruit, squash, lilac, phlox, and roses. It also helps to prevent black spot on roses. Dissolve a tablespoon in a gallon of water and add a half-teaspoon of liquid soap to act as a carrying agent, then spray after plants have leafed out but *before* signs appear. You can add a tablespoon of light horticultural oil to the mix to smother any fungal spores present.

Cornmeal

Cornmeal foils fungal diseases. Work 2 pounds of cornmeal into every 100 square feet of garden where fungal diseases (molds, for example) are a concern, or make a spray by soaking a cup of cornmeal in a gallon of water for several hours, then straining the liquid. Horticultural-grade cornmeal is less expensive than food grade, but either type works, and both can help add nutrients to the soil.

CHAPTER 7

CHEAP SKILLS

What sets the best gardeners apart from the average ones? Believe it or not, the answer is not money. A hefty budget certainly helps cover up mistakes; you can always throw out a dead plant and put in a new one. But what really separates the great gardeners from average ones is knowledge and skill.

Knowledge comes from reading, talking to other gardeners, and good old-fashioned experience. Skill is just knowledge in action. Put what you learn into practice, and watch it pay off.

Read and Learn

You don't need to squander a fortune on gardening books or magazines. That's why libraries exist. Of course, some books (this one, for example!) are valuable references you may want to keep close at hand. Clip interesting magazine articles, and keep them in a scrapbook. Above all, keep reading. Something new is always sprouting in the gardening world.

Digging Around Online

The largest free library in the world is literally at your fingertips. You can join online communities, search Web sites (see Resources), shop for supplies, and even take courses. Internet information may be much more up-to-date than even the most current periodical, but don't assume that it is.

If you're not a fan of reading a computer monitor for hours, don't forget that there is another, much more intuitive learning tool online — video. The YouTube explosion has put mini-tutorials for almost any skill imaginable at your fingertips.

Keeping Good Records

A helpful habit that really pays off is record keeping. Keep a record of annual first and last frost dates. Record what you plant, the variety, how much (including the number of seeds or square footage) you plant, days to *actual* harvest, amount of harvest, and any other pertinent information. Remember the importance of crop rotation. Draw a diagram, and write down what crops you planted where.

By comparing this information annually, you will eventually fine-tune your gardening practices to perfectly suit your situation. Well-kept records will also show you exactly where you spend your gardening dollars. Set a goal each year to cut costs in at least one of your gardening-expense areas.

Photos are a great way to document your garden layout, as well as its health and productivity from year to year. You may notice, for instance, that tomatoes do better at the south end of your garden than at the north, or that carrots planted with peas matured faster than those in a bed by themselves. If you use a computer, you can take digital photos and keep files without worrying about the cost per photo. If you use standard film and have it developed, you'll want to make each image count. Either way, hard copies of your garden photos, arranged in a computer program or in a scrapbook, will give you unimpeachable evidence of your garden's progress.

GREEN THUMB

You Can't Afford Not to Mulch

Mulching saves money on irrigation, weed killers, and, depending on the mulch you use, fertilizer, not to mention disposal fees for yard debris. Mulching cuts down on the time you spend weeding and cultivating, and it boosts harvests. If you don't already use this cost-cutting technique in your garden, now is the time to begin.

▶ **To prevent any growth at all,** such as for a dry riverbed feature or a walkway, inorganic mulches such as weed-barrier fabric or rocks work well. These can be a lot of work to put down and are meant to stay in place indefinitely, so apply weed killer or a preemergent herbicide before placing the mulch to insure nothing pokes up through it.

▶ **To prevent growth in some areas** while encouraging it in others, such as around landscape specimens, an organic mulch such as shredded bark might be a better choice. Water will penetrate and reach the roots of the established plants, but weeds will find it tougher to get a foothold.

▶ **To foster crop growth while foiling weeds,** an organic mulch such as compost or straw is great because it slowly nourishes plants while performing all the other duties of mulch.

Money-Saving Mulches

Note: The levels recommended here are deeper than many people use, but too little mulch won't create an effective barrier against weeds.

Alfalfa
Depth: 6"   Frequency of Application: Every year
Pros and Cons: Excellent mulch. Contains the plant growth hormone triacontanol, high in nitrogen, and trace minerals. Not very attractive.
Find It Cheap: Buy low-quality, old, rain-damaged, or partially rotted alfalfa hay (it's less attractive to animals and farmers and fine for mulch).

Bark, shredded
Depth: 3-4"   Frequency of Application : Every other year
Pros and Cons: Attractive, decomposes slowly, burns nitrogen as it degrades.
Find It Cheap: Landscape-supply companies. Cheaper by the cubic yard than in bags, so if you don't need a full truckload, see if you can find a friend or neighbor to split expenses.

Compost
Depth: 4"   Frequency of Application: Annually
Pros and Cons: Excellent; feeds soil.
Find It Cheap: Your compost pile.

Grass clippings
Depth: 4-6" dried or composted or 1 inch fresh
Frequency of Application: Annually
Pros and Cons: If not dried first, will clump and mat. Be sure they are herbicide free.
Find It Cheap: Rake from your own or neighbors' lawns.

MORE

Money-Saving Mulches (continued)

Gravel

Depth: 2–4"   Frequency of Application: Once

Pros and Cons: Decorative and allows for free flow of water, but also lets weeds through. Contributes no organic material. Absorbs heat, which can affect shallow roots. Best if applied over another type of mulch.

Find It Cheap: Landscape suppliers; priced by the ton.

Landscape fabric

Depth: Single layer   Frequency of Application: Every 3 to 5 years

Pros and Cons: Allows water and air through freely. Works best around shrubs or under landscape features; expensive and a pain to dig up and replace.

Find It Cheap: Landscape companies, home improvement stores.

Leaves, shredded

Depth: 4–6"   Frequency of Application: Annually

Pros and Cons: Adds organic matter and trace minerals. Good mulch.

Find It Cheap: Collect your neighbors' (you may even get paid to take them!).

Newspaper

Depth: Several layers   Frequency of Application : Annually

Pros and Cons: Good weed barrier, great between rows of vegetables, but unsightly.

Find It Cheap: Collect from neighbors or local dump or recycling center.

Pine Needles

Depth: 3–4"   Frequency of Application: Every 2 or 3 years

Pros and Cons: Decomposes slowly; smothers weeds; won't compact. Slightly acidic.

Find It Cheap: In some areas, people might pay you to take them!

Plastic

Depth: Single layer   **Frequency of Application:** Every 2 to 3 seasons

Pros and Cons: All colors warm soil and retain soil moisture, but black is best at smothering weeds. Best around vegetables.

Find It Cheap: Salvage from packaging. Use big sheets or overlap smaller pieces.

Salt hay

Depth: 3–6"   **Frequency of Application:** Annually

Pros and Cons: Great for pathways and vegetables. Doesn't mat, seed free; avoid grass hay — it's loaded with seeds.

Find It Cheap: Gather from fields, or purchase at feed stores.

Straw

Depth: 6–8"   **Frequency of Application:** Annually

Pros and Cons: Light and easy to work with. Adds organic matter when tilled in. Great around veggies or over lawn seed.

Find It Cheap: Buy from a farmer or a feed store. Partially rotted is as good as fresh for mulching and is often free.

Wood chips, shavings, or sawdust

Depth: 3–4"   **Frequency of Application:** Annually

Pros and Cons: Add a cup of 21-0-0 or ½ cup 43-0-0 per 100 feet to counter nitrogen depletion.

Find It Cheap: Sawmills; landscape supply companies.

Using Plastic Mulches

Plastic mulch is an effective way manipulate growing conditions by magnifying the sun's heat to warm up soil. For most crops it is best to mulch in the spring *after* the soil warms up, because it helps to retain soil warmth. Heat-loving crops, such as melons and peppers, really benefit from toasty feet. Mulch cool-loving crops, such as spinach or broccoli, earlier in the growing season to keep the soil cool near their roots.

Although black plastic itself heats up more than clear, clear plastic transmits more heat through to the soil if left uncovered. Red-tinted plastic mulch, called Selective Reflecting Mulch or SRM-Red, stymies weeds and warms soil like black plastic, and in university tests it actually boosted production of early tomatoes. It works by reflecting red light waves back into the plants, and they react with phytochrome pigments to stimulate growth. Some studies suggest the same results in strawberries.

But is the difference enough to warrant the higher price? The answer seems to depend on how much sun your garden gets and the temperature. Tests in South Carolina showed increases of 12 to 20 percent, similar to tests in Montana, but tests in Pennsylvania showed that blue-colored plastic did a better job than red.

Raise Your Beds, Not Your Expenses

To create inexpensive, efficient, and good-looking raised beds, all you need is a shovel. If the plot has not already been cultivated, rent a rototiller first to break up the ground and till in amendments. You can make the beds any shape or length. Leave about 18 inches between them to allow enough room for you to work, and be sure to incorporate an extra-wide row every so often to accommodate your wheelbarrow or garden cart.

MORE

DIRT CHEAP

Some gardeners have a long, hard row to hoe, while others work in raised beds. Gardening in raised beds has several economic advantages over rows in a flat plot. The growing beds are separate from pathways, so you can apply fertilizers and soil amendments only where needed, which eliminates waste.

Soil in raised beds does not compact and is easy to work by hand, eliminating rototiller expense. Crops can be grown close together, which maximizes the harvest return for the space used. Raised beds create better drainage, and the increased surface area causes the soil to warm quickly in the spring, increasing the production of flowers and vegetables alike.

To save money, construct beds from landscape timbers, hewn logs, cement blocks, brick, stone, or any suitable material that's already on hand. As with containers, avoid using treated or painted lumber. The least expensive beds, however, are freestanding.

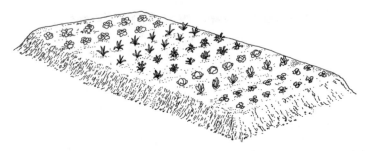

Make the beds narrow enough to plant or weed from either side without ever having to step into the prepared soil. This prevents plant-stunting soil compaction that is inevitable in row gardens. I find 30 to 36 inches a good width and 12 feet long a convenient length.

Once the layout is complete, shovel the topsoil from the pathways, along with liberal amounts of compost or other organic soil amendments, into the beds. This puts the best soil where it will do the most good, while elevating the soil level in the beds. With a rake flatten the topsoil in the beds.

GREEN THUMB

For maximum efficiency maintain your raised beds in the same spot every year. Mulch or add manure in the fall to shield the surface from windborne weed seeds and insects. Check the beds early in the spring, and if you keep chickens, turn them out in the garden to seek out and destroy soil-dwelling insects. Due to improved drainage and warmth, beds will be ready to plant sooner than you may expect. Spade, rake, and start planting!

Train to Gain

Another cheap skill that can really improve garden output is trellising. This practice utilizes vertical space by training otherwise ground-hogging crops to climb a support. Since trellised plants cover less ground space, they use water more efficiently, are less work to weed, receive more sunlight, have better disease-preventing air circulation, and are easier to manage for pest control. All of this adds up to increased yields with less input and expense.

Cheap and Easy Trellising

All you need to trellis a vining plant is a support that may or may not require a framework. Some vines will scramble up the support unaided, while others need to be periodically positioned and tied into place.

As with raised beds, the setup can be more expensive than the crop is worth. But you don't need to overspend on trellises. Inexpensive trellises work as well as expensive ones — and even the cheapest trellis looks wonderful covered in healthy green or flowering vines. If the support is strong, the plants will supply the beauty. Here are some easy, inexpensive ways to train your plants:

MORE ▶

▶ **Stretch a sturdy line between two support posts** and tie strands of twine to it for pole beans. Once the bean seedlings reach the ends of the strands, they *grab on* and climb up, quickly hiding the twine. Weave twine between the posts to train other vines.

▶ **Suspend a section of salvaged fencing between posts,** or dangle it from an eave, and watch it vanish from view as green growth covers it. Welded or woven-wire fencing works well.

▶ **Set up teepees of bamboo poles** and let climbing vines transform them into green pyramids.

GREEN THUMB

For permanent fixtures such as climbing roses, the main consideration is an accessible support. Long-lived vines require pruning and other maintenance that annual crops don't need. If trellises are near the house, keep them at least a foot from the walls to allow for adequate ventilation, as well as maintenance to the vine and house.

Consider that some vining plants, such as wisteria, become very heavy with age and require strong supports. A rambler rose weaving through an old apple tree is a glorious sight, but vines and trees must compete for food, water, and light. Make sure both plants receive what they need.

Easy Trellising

Build your trellises for convenience as well as cost. A favorite of mine is a ladder-style A-frame made of 1-inch by 2-inch lumber and hinged at the top. It will support any vining plant from beans to cantaloupe, lasts for years,

A-frame trellis

and flattens easily for storage. In the winter, you can bring this trellis indoors and use it as a clothes-drying rack.

Some Plants Suitable for Trellising

Blackberry	Grape	Raspberry
Bougainvillea	Honeysuckle	Scarlet runner bean
Cantaloupe	Jasmine	Sweet potato
Clematis	Melon	Tomato
Climbing rose	Passionflower	Trumpet vine
Cucumber	Pole bean	Wisteria

Easy post frame

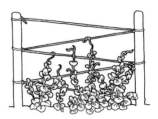

Posts with horizontal twine

Prune and Pinch More than Pennies

Pruning is the brave act of cutting off parts of a plant in the hope of making it better. It may be hard, but it works and it's worth it! Pruning makes plants more vigorous by concentrating growth into the remaining stems. It controls the shape, flowering, or fruiting of plants. It also makes them healthier by eliminating weak or diseased stems and allowing more light and air to reach remaining stems and foliage.

Principles of Pruning

Here are some basic pruning rules that apply to all plants. These are very general guidelines, compared with the volumes written on precise pruning and training techniques. But if you never do more than what is mentioned here, you will still improve your investment. For best results, learn about your specific plants.

1. Remove dead or diseased wood; cut below the soil line if possible. You can tell if a stem is dead by scraping the bark with a sharp knife. If the tissue beneath the bark is green, then the branch is alive. If it is yellow, the stem is alive but ailing. If you find brown or grey colors, then the branch is dead. Diseased wood may have cankers, which are dark, depressed spots. Diseased wood also may show blotches, spots, or other obvious signs of illness.

2. Cut off spindly, overcrowded, or poorly placed stems flush with the main branch.

3. Finally, you may have to remove some limbs just because there are too many growing for a healthy plant to support. How many stems to remove depends on the plant and your desired results. For instance, prune cane fruits, such as raspberries, back to no more than seven or eight canes on one plant; more canes lower fruit production. Another example is the hybrid tea rose. If you remove more stems, they produce fewer but larger flowers.

4. Once you remove extraneous stems, many plants need the remaining branches shortened. Some plants, such as many varieties of clematis and passionflower, can be cut back to the ground. For some others remove only the tips to spur new growth.

MORE

DIRT CHEAP

Don't spend money on wound-dressing ointments. A properly made pruning cut will heal itself. There is no clear evidence that dressings reduce wood rot associated with pruning. Proper cuts reduce damage.

Pruning Pointers

To start pruning, all you need is a pair of gloves and a good set of pruning shears or a sharp knife. For larger branches you need a pair of loppers, perhaps a saw, and a working knowledge of the particular plant. Some plants flower or fruit on the current year's growth, others on year-old wood, and some on wood of different ages. Knowing which stems are the productive ones is crucial to a good pruning job. Otherwise you may cut off limbs that are about to flower.

Timing is also important. Early spring is a good time to remove old or dead wood and shape species that flower on year-old wood. Wait until after the shrubs have flowered, however, to cut them back. Prune plants that bloom on the current season's growth in late spring or early winter, and those that bloom on old wood only after the blooms (and fruit) have come and gone for the season.

Every cut you make will have a consequence. If you prune above a bud, it will sprout and grow in the direction it faces.

Cut at a slant above and away from the chosen bud, ⅛ to ¼ inch above it. The last bud on the stem becomes the leader or the new end of the stem.

Prune in Early Spring

Climbers

Anemone clematis
Bougainvillea
Hoya
Hydrangea, climbing
Jasmine
Rambler rose
Wisteria

Shrubs

Cotoneaster
Forsythia
Italian jasmine

Prune in Early Winter/Late Spring

Climbers

Clematis, large-flowered
Climbing rose
Grapes
Honeysuckle
Passionflower
Plumbago
Trumpet vine

Shrubs

Butterfly bush
Hardy fuchsia
Hibiscus
Hydrangea ('Annabelle' and
  other arborescens)
Spirea, western

Prune after Blooming

Hydrangea, lacecap and
  mophead
Lilac
Mock orange
Weigela

Thinning to Increase Yield

Many plants and trees, especially dwarf fruit varieties, produce more, bigger, and healthier fruit if thinned. It's also the best way to prevent young trees from over-producing so much that the tree becomes bent for life. Also, overproducing one year often results in a small harvest the next.

▶ **Apples.** Pinch out apple blossoms or wait until after the "June drop," when trees naturally drop imperfect fruit. Thin fruit to an average of 6 inches apart.

▶ **Apricots.** When fruits are just under an inch wide, thin to 4 to 6 inches apart, starting with any damaged or unhealthy fruits first.

▶ **Cherries.** These trees don't require thinning.

▶ **Citrus.** These can bear enough fruit to break their limbs if not thinned. After natural fruit drop, thin a little at a time, focusing on damaged or unhealthy fruit first. Thin so that fruit is evenly spaced on the tree, on robust limbs.

▶ **Grapes.** Remove smallest flower clusters from grapevines, leaving about a foot between remaining bunches. Snip off parts of developing bunches to create that classic grape-cluster shape and to improve the size and quality of the still-forming individual grapes. If the cluster is in the shade, pull off a leaf or two as the grapes begin to ripen to increase the amount of sunlight the grapes receive.

▶ **Peaches and nectarines.** Early in the season thin to one fruit from each cluster. Space fruits from 6 to 9 inches apart during the season.

▶ **Pears.** Thin pears to one or two per cluster, after the natural fruit drop.

▶ **Plums.** Thin large-fruited cultivars of plums, leaving 3 to 4 inches between fruit. Thin small-fruited varieties, leaving 2 to 3 inches between fruit.

Many blooming shrubs form thick tangles of spindly growth unless pruned annually. Regular thinning promotes strong, new growth from the base of the plant. It also prevents the loss of bloom quality that accompanies twiggy growth.

Not all plants require hours of pruning, however. Many plants, such as the flowering pagoda dogwood, daphne, camellia, hibiscus, and deciduous viburnum, prosper with minimal pruning.

GREEN THUMB

Practice Pinching

A good pinch now and then is one of the best methods for producing full-blooming plants. Pinching out growing tips on perennials and annuals early in the season causes the plant to develop lateral buds lower on the plant. These buds fill in to give the plant a full, bushy shape. They also develop more flower buds, and when the plant comes into bloom, there are more blossoms.

▶ **For branching perennials** such as rudbeckia and chrysanthemum, wait until the plant is about one-third of its mature size. Pinch back the top 1 or 2 inches of each shoot. The ones you pinch first will bloom first, so spread this job over a few days to increase the plant's flowering time.

Pinching out growing tips encourages growth of buds below.

▶ **Pinch back annuals** such as petunias that tend to get leggy if left alone. Snap them off at a joint. This is also a good trick to force a bed of plants into uniform growth. Pinching removes the buds that would have bloomed first and delays flowering. You may want to leave a few buds intact for early color and pinch them after the rest of the flowers are in bloom.

▶ **Deadheading, or removing spent blossoms,** is a necessary evil for flowering plants. Pinch or cut out dead flowers before the plant begins to put its energy into producing seeds, to encourage the plant to keep flowering.

GREEN THUMB

Disbudding is a form of pinching that produces outstanding blossoms. You can trick flowers that tend to bloom in bunches — such as dahlias, certain roses, and chrysanthemums — into producing one outstanding bloom where they would have produced several less-dazzling flowers. Choose the largest (usually the center) bud, and pinch out all others to the stem. This forces the plant's energy into producing that one perfect bloom.

CHAPTER 8

LANDSCAPE FOR LESS

What makes some gardens so irresistible? Often it's a cunning focal point or a clever use of plants. A cheap garden doesn't have to look plain or tacky. On the contrary, the fascinating finds that some frugal gardeners incorporate into their plots often call for a second look. It's easy to create a focal point or a functional addition to your garden with nothing more than your imagination and instinct.

Think Like a Plant

Perhaps the biggest rule of garden recycling is to learn to think like a plant, sort of. Plants don't care how their needs are met, as long as they are met. Climbers need something to climb on, specimen plants need room to show off, and everything needs to be watered.

A used or recycled gardening find may not look all that pretty at first, but can be camouflaged with a little extra thought, effort, or just some old-fashioned time and patience. An old stock watering tank becomes an attractive, self-contained raised bed when painted or disguised behind lattice-work, then filled with soil and compost.

If the appearance of plastic milk jugs leaking into your tomato plants embarrasses you, simply bury the jugs and save money proudly! If appearances can wait, an ugly PVC trellis, fence, or old bed frame will look better as climbing vines cover any sign of the unsightly support.

Finders Cheapers

An important consideration when looking for inexpensive accessories is personal taste. Unless you are trying to make a point, nothing should stand out in your garden more than your plants. For instance, most gardeners prefer that plant supports not show after the plants have grown to their mature size. Some great finds, however, such as a weathered old wooden step-ladder, blend into the garden scheme wonderfully as obvious plant supports.

Rules for Recycling

As a thrifty gardener you should always look for free or cheap items to use in your garden. One person's trash is another person's trellis. Follow these rules for recycling:

▶ Make sure any material you find to use in a vegetable garden is free of toxins.

▶ Don't make rain barrels out of anything that once contained any form of poison, including petroleum products.

▶ Don't use railroad ties or landscape timbers that have been treated with a lead-based paint or a wood preservative, other than copper napthenate.

▶ Don't use old tires for growing food — chemical residues in the tire may leach into the crops.

DIRT CHEAP

I'm not suggesting you have a junkyard theme, but many fabulous finds await you in items other people have thrown away. All it takes is imagination and a little time searching out great finds. Many municipal landfills have a separate area for furniture and household items, along with construction debris and other materials. Yard and garage sales are a terrific source for planters, plant supports, even garden furniture. Look for a building "re-store" in your area that recycles construction materials.

Create a rustic-looking arbor, trellis, or tomato cage with natural branches. Fresh-cut saplings or pliant green limbs of willow, alder, poplar, and cottonwood are excellent raw material for bentwood projects from trellises to furniture. (See Resources, starting on page 269 in the Appendix section, for more ideas).

You can turn an old piece of farm machinery, a beached rowboat, or an old gate into a garden centerpiece with plants growing in, around, and through it. Old wagon wheels are popular garden props; you can recreate the look by sectioning a round herb garden with spokes made of thick wooden dowels or evenly sized, trimmed branches.

Use an old wooden ladder to create a neatly partitioned herb garden or flower bed, perhaps along a walkway or by the side of a garage or shed. Gnarled driftwood, large stones, and other natural items make wonderful centerpieces or borders.

Set a Spell

After all your hard work, you want to sit and enjoy the sights and scents. For those with the tools, time, and skill, building an attractive garden bench from a kit or a plan makes a fine project. Use redwood or cedar for a weather-resistant bench, and coat with a wood preservative. Pine is cheaper but needs staining and regular upkeep to stay looking nice.

If you do opt to splurge on a store-bought bench, go with wrought iron — it will probably outlast the garden. Hardwood benches can cost several times as much and may not last nearly as long.

You can substitute many items for a traditional garden bench. Old wicker furniture fits well into a garden theme; use an air compressor or stiff brush to remove flaking old paint, then repaint and finish with a sealant. Thick sections of unsplit logs can serve as unobtrusive garden perches. For a softer settee settle yourself on a bale of hay or straw, but toss a cover over it if you are wearing shorts!

DIRT CHEAP

Need more seating ideas? Check out *www.freebenchplans.com* or *www.backyardspaces.com* for free garden-bench plans online. Most of the plans include cost-to-build estimates.

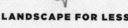

*If you have some planks —
preferably sanded and
coated with varnish for
a smooth, long-lasting
sitting surface — and two
sections of post, you have
the materials for a bench.*

*Sink the posts into the
ground so the tops reach a comfortable height for sitting, around 2 feet high.
Fasten a piece of board with 2-inch or larger wood screws
to each post, and attach planks to these boards lengthwise. The
dimensions depend on the materials available and your needs.*

*This is a very plain, rustic bench. But a few potted plants,
clinging vines, or flowering plants will transform it into a work
of beauty.*

*My favorite garden bench looked like Fred Flintstone made it. It
was built from a 5-foot-long section of log split lengthwise, and two
2-foot lengths of the same tree. The 2-foot sections were carved to
fit snugly against the rounded side of the log, and it was solid.*

Birdbath Basics

Provided you keep them out of the berry patch, birds add so much to the garden and ask very little in return. One surefire way to draw their attention is to provide them with a source of water, a necessity for other beneficial organisms as well.

An old aluminum garbage can lid, turned over, holds water wonderfully. Set it on the ground, a few feet from any plants that may provide cat cover. Scatter a little gravel on the bottom of the lid for footing, and fill with water. Arrange a few stones or overflowing plants around the rim to disguise the lid's true identity. If you prefer an elevated birdbath, hang the lid in a rope sling, pad the sling with moss, and nestle the lid into it for a decorative effect.

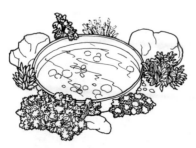

You can create a birdbath from an old aluminum garbage can lid. Either sink it in the ground in a quiet spot or hang it from a sling padded with moss.

Build a stonelike birdbath by mixing equal parts portland cement, milled peat moss, and mason sand with just enough water to make it cling together; this mixture is called hypertufa.

1. Pour the mixture into a plastic-lined mold, such as an old birdbath or a garbage can lid, about 1½ inches thick against the bottom and edges.

2. Let dry a day or two, then remove the plastic, and stress the exposed edge for a hewn-stone look. Or chip it with a chisel, hack with a hatchet, and scrub with a wire brush for the realistic look of handcarved stone.

3. Set aside in a warm, dry spot to cure for four to six weeks.

4. Finish curing for another few weeks in the weather to neutralize the cement. Frequent watering helps leach out chemicals.

5. Give it a final rinse with vinegar to neutralize alkalinity.

Pondering a Pond?

Something about the reflective serenity of a garden pond draws visitors to pause and ponder. It provides moisture and a cool refuge for beneficial insects, birds, and animals. And it opens a whole new class of plant possibilities to the gardener.

A simple pond can be as low maintenance as it is inexpensive. Fancier versions with pumps and lights require more attention and of course cost more. Simplicity is both beautiful and cheap.

There are two types of do-it-yourself installation kits available. One type consists of a premolded rigid liner, and you dig a hole to fit the container. The other type uses a flexible plastic-sheet liner, which offers the creative freedom of fitting the liner to the hole.

Flexible liners are less bulky, as well as less expensive. They allow you to create underwater shelves, 9 to 12 inches wide and 9 to 12 inches below the surface, to simulate realistic conditions for pond plants and fish. Also, flexible liners allow you to angle the bottom deeper at one end, which causes debris to settle in one spot.

Either one makes a lovely garden pond. The basic steps for installation are the same.

1. To prepare the pond, first mark the outline with a rope or garden hose, then score around the outline with a shovel or spade.

2. Dig to the depth your pond will be, plus 3 inches (for a layer of sand). Most water-garden plants need at least 6 inches of water, and pond fish, such as goldfish or koi, require a deep end of at least 24 inches as a place to hibernate. If you plan to stock fish in the pond, use a fish-grade liner.

3. Span the hole with a board, and rest a level on top. Make any adjustments necessary to keep the pond edges level.

4. Shovel in a 3-inch cushion of damp sand, and settle the liner in place.

DIRT CHEAP

You can substitute other materials for either type of pond for added savings. Use thick black plastic in place of the flexible liner (not recommended with fish), or sink a kid's pool as you would a rigid liner. Since landscape plants, arranged stones, water plants, and dirt settling to the bottom obscure the pond liner from view, no one will ever know the difference. Large-sized kids' pools go on sale at the end of the summer for a fraction of their original cost.

Looking Good Enough to Eat

Savvy use of your favorite plants goes a long way toward creating your dream garden, and I don't merely mean having a well-arranged layout, although that is always pleasing. I mean making your plants and your invested dollars pull double duty. For example, if you need an attractive plant to fill in a border, cover an unsightly fence, or act as a screen, why not choose food?

Veggies Add Visual Flair

Many edible plants can make a bold visual statement. The fernlike growth of asparagus adds a delicate touch, for example. The large leaves of rhubarb and its contrasting stems are a fountain of drama, as are smaller, no less striking strains of colored Swiss chard.

Artichokes lend an almost mystical image, Oregon grape a hint of woodlands, and purple bush beans a bit of whimsy. Purple cabbage and ornamental kale make bold centerpieces or can be planted in rows or groupings. Bright red, orange, and yellow hot peppers spice up the border in more ways than one.

Still other edibles blend their texture, shape, and green healthy leaves into the overall tapestry of your yard. The large blue-green leaves of broccoli, feathery heads of fennel, lacy leaves of dill, ruffles of salad greens and lettuce, curls of kale, glossy ribbons of spinach, or the frills of green and purple basil fill in splendidly around, beneath, or behind more colorful plants.

Flowers Do Double Duty

Reconsider some of the plants you normally think of as "ornamental." Lots of flowers are edible, including borage, violets, pansies, nasturtiums, sunflowers, and daylilies. And some plants just do it all. Roses not only lend a romantic flair but also provide petals for salads, desserts, and punch, as well as nutritious, tangy rose hips for a burst of citrus flavor and vitamin C in teas, jams, and jellies. One big rugosa rose hip has 60 times more vitamin C than an orange.

Edible Ornamentals

Ground Covers	Vines/Screens/Hedges
Cranberry	Beans (V)
Creeping thyme	Blackberry (V)
Lemon balm	Blueberry (H)
Lingonberry	Cucumber (V)
Low-bush blueberry	Currant (H)
Oregano	Gooseberry (H)
Parsley	Grapes (V)
Prostrate rosemary	Hardy kiwi (V)
Roman chamomile	Raspberry (S, H)
Salad greens	Rugosa rose (H)
Strawberry	Squash (V)
Wintergreen	Tomato (V, S)
	Watermelon (V)

KEY: (G) Ground Cover; (H) Hedge; (P) Perennial; (S) Shrub; (V)Vine

If you are planting fruit trees, you can add a touch of fantasy for no extra cost by espaliering (training to various shapes) apples, pears, plums, or gooseberries into living sculptures or fences. All it takes is a plan of the finished look, some pinching back, and the patience to wait through several growing seasons.

GREEN THUMB

For more immediate results, grow vining miniature tomatoes in window boxes or hanging baskets. Decorate a porch or patio with containers of herbs, greens, peppers, or blueberries, or drape hanging vines of cantaloupe, green beans, or grapes over an arbor or awning.

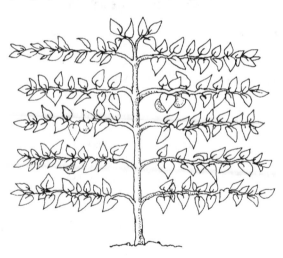

Horizontal T cordon espalier

A Year-Round Investment

The garden has more to offer than just pretty spring and summer blooms. Consider including a few plants that offer a point of interest beyond the first act — go for the curtain call!

Many plants put on a splendid show in the fall, even after they've bloomed. Let fiery-colored leaves and bright berries decorate your autumn surroundings. The red leaves of *Spiraea japonica,* purples of flowering plums, and yellows of the maidenhair tree all play the same role as flowers in the summer garden. Berries, in white (snowberry), red (cotoneaster, holly), orange (mountain ash), and dusky purple (Oregon grape), contribute their own thousand points of light.

MORE

Create a Winter Wonderland

Plants providing winter interest give your garden morale a boost when you least expect it but need it most. Gardeners value many types of roses, including rugosas, antique "Old Garden" varieties, and the cultivar 'Geranium' for the bright orange to red hips they produce. Not only are they attractive, but also they provide welcome winter food for birds. The ptericantha rose has enormous, bright red, inch-wide thorns that become visible after the foliage drops.

Evergreen shrubs, such as Oregon grape, hollies, junipers and *Euonymus,* retain their good looks throughout the winter. Try redtwig or yellowtwig dogwood, white-stemmed *Rubus biflorus* or the twisted branches of the contorted European filbert for colorful winter appeal. Use climbers, such as winter-blooming jasmine or evergreen ivies, to accentuate the winter garden.

Hedging on Fences

Let's say you want a line of demarcation to mark your territory. A lesser gardener might think of an ordinary old fence. But let the creative force in you take over, and you may find a better, and perhaps cheaper, alternative.

Hedges are popular on property lines for many reasons. They look quite nice when properly maintained, and they keep most people on their own side. A negative aspect is the amount of upkeep. The time and expense of trimming and maintaining a hedge is not a real selling point. But what if that hedge required very little upkeep and offered more than just a boundary line?

Beyond Boxwood

Whoever said hedges have to be of boxwood or privet, especially when there are other plants with so much more to offer? Consider some of the following plants for hedges:

Blueberry. Produces lovely white flowers in spring, luscious berries in summer, and attractive red foliage in fall.

Fruit trees. Grow apple, pear, peach, plum, or cherry trees in a two-dimensional shape on a trellis. Train the arms, or cordons, of the trees into interlocking patterns to create a

MORE

living fence. Each tree can span 6 to 8 feet of "fence line" and will take from three to six years to reach its full potential, depending on how complicated a pattern you undertake.

Grapes. Fast-growing vines quickly cover a trellis to form a wall of green, attractive leaves and sumptuous grapes. Plant so the south side is on your side of the property line; this is where the most fruit forms.

Hawthorne. Provides fragrant flowers, fruit, and fall foliage, as well as enough thorns to keep out snoopy neighbors.

Holly. Stays attractive year-round, forms an impenetrable wall, and even provides Christmas decorations.

Rugosa and shrub roses. Perfume the air and supply armloads of romantic bouquets and hips for jelly.

Dirt Cheap

Materials for fencing can be very expensive, but a cheap alternative is waiting for you. Warehouses throw away damaged wooden pallets every day. Collect matching pallets, erect them around the garden, and paint if desired. If done well, the humble beginnings of such a garden fence only adds to its rustic charm. Or you can plant a few vines to disguise it.

A Good Fence Makes Good Sense

Sometimes having a fence is a necessity. If you want to contain pets or children, it's a must. A fence camouflaged by a hedge or plant provides more than just privacy. Dense vegetation will buffer sound and will make your garden a quieter place. Use plants to block an unattractive view, hide the compost pile, or create a gardener's refuge.

Inexpensive fencing doesn't have to be ugly, however. Use it as a backdrop, and let climbing plants flow over it in a cascade of color and fragrance. Transform a lowly chain-link fence with blossom-bursting annual vines of trailing nasturtium, sweet pea, or morning glories.

Put the fence to work supporting a crop of pole beans or garden peas. Perennial vines, such as clematis, climbing rose, trumpet vine, and scores of others, turn a fence into a yearly delight.

For a solid wood fence, you can resort to ivies or tack up a few horizontal wires to support other climbers. If you happen to be on the south side of the fence, take advantage of this warmth-creating microclimate. Paint it white, and use the space to grow cold-tender plants or fabulous fruit.

CHAPTER 9

LONGER LIFE FOR YOUR PLANT DOLLARS

Unless you garden in the tropics, you probably have wished there was just a little more to the growing season. After all, you can only stomach so many green tomatoes. Take heart — no matter what zone you live in, you *can* lengthen the growing season in your garden, using inexpensive season extenders. You can also extend and protect the life of tender landscape plants.

Hot Caps
Equal Cold Cash

Hot caps are flimsy little wax-paper plant covers sold in garden stores. When placed over transplants, they protect from light frost. They are inexpensive and do the job, but there are even cheaper substitutes.

When making hot caps or cloches (the generic name for frost-protective plant coverings), use material that will allow sunlight through. Young plants need light to grow, and the covering magnifies the warm air surrounding the transplants. On the morning after a frost, a temperature difference of just a few degrees often makes the difference between a thriving plant and a dead one.

Leave the coverings on the plant after the danger of frost has passed, to encourage more vigorous plant growth in the warm, moist microclimate. Remove them as the plants outgrow them or as the days get warmer.

Fight Frost for Free

▶ **Clear, plastic 2-liter bottles** (#1 recycle symbol) make great substitutes for store-bought hot caps for individual plants. Remove the labels that would otherwise block sunlight, then cut the bottom out of each bottle. Save the caps.

At planting time, position a bottle (with the cap on) over each tender transplant. Push the cut end down into the soil to anchor it, being careful not to cut into transplant roots.

If your garden gets a lot of wind, tap two stakes into the ground with the transplant, angled just enough to help stabilize the lightweight bottle. Remove when the plant leaves crowd the edges of the bottle. The bottles nest together for convenient storage.

▶ **Opaque plastic 1-gallon bottles** (#2 recycle symbol), such as those containing distilled water or milk, work as well as or better than the 2-liter size. Their biggest advantage is size — plants don't outgrow them as quickly. They also come with a built-in anchor support. Cut the top out of the handle,

Homemade hot caps from 2-liter soda bottles and a gallon jug

push a thin stake or piece of bamboo through, and anchor in the soil.

▶ **Wire tomato cages** also make good plant protectors. Position them over the plant, and cover with one or two clear-plastic bags. These will accommodate a fairly large plant. Remember to ventilate the cover on sunny days. Wait until the dew dries, and pull off the plastic or open it up to the air. Replace the cover in late afternoon so that it can reheat before nightfall.

DIRT CHEAP

I like plastic-bottle cloches better than their commercial cousins for two reasons. One reason is that they are free. The other is that you can unscrew the cap to vent the covering on sunny days. This is important, because heat can build up inside the covering and scorch young plants.

Some store-bought plant protectors are worth the ticket price. Sold as Wall-O-Water, Season Starter, and Kozy Coat, they run about $10 for a three-pack (shop around, as prices vary by as much as $6, and some suppliers offer quantity discounts). All these protectors convert sunlight into warmth by day, store it, and release it at night, protecting transplants from below-freezing temperatures. If properly cared for, they will last for years. Repair kits are sold for less than $2.

Recycled Row Covers

Sometimes it's not practical to cover each individual transplant, and you need to construct some sort of protection for entire rows or beds. Make it a habit throughout the year to collect clear scrap plastic to make larger covers.

Dry-cleaning bags are thin but serviceable; use at least two layers. Large, heavy-duty plastic bags used to cover furniture, mattresses, bedding, and some appliances are a great find, and by reusing them you are doing an added service by keeping them out of landfills.

How to Build Them

Bend light-duty, ½-inch PVC pipe, bamboo stakes, fresh-cut saplings, or sections of wire mesh over rows or beds, and push the ends into the soil to anchor them. Most types of wire mesh will hold their shape freestanding over the width of garden beds, but hoops made of other materials will try to bend back to their original shape, so you may need to anchor them, especially if your soil is loose.

To make a sturdy base for your hoops, drive 1- or 2-foot sections of pipe into the ground every 2 feet on both sides of the bed, and slip the hoops' ends inside the pipe. Cut your hoop material about 2 feet longer to allow for anchoring.

The force of the material resisting being bent will hold it upright and in place. Whatever material you use, make sure it is strong enough and anchored sufficiently to withstand the prevailing winds when covered with plastic.

PVC Tips

Black PVC, sold in coils, is cheaper and more flexible than schedule 40, white PVC pipe. To bend pipe larger than half an inch or to create a permanent curve that won't try to snap back to its original shape, use a heat gun to make it more malleable. Work in a well-ventilated area, as PVC emits toxic fumes at high temperatures, and wear gloves and eye protection. Once it cools, the pipe will retain its new shape.

You can also buy pipe-spring-bender gizmos that let you bend thicknesses of ½-, ¾- and 1-inch PVC without heat while still maintaining the integrity of the pipe.

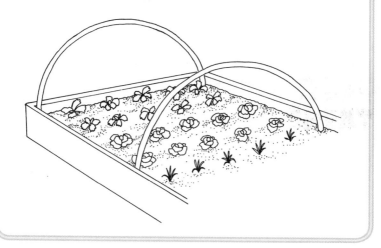

Fighting That First Frost

The first frost catches many gardeners off guard and effectively ends the growing season, even though weeks of warm, sunny days may follow. Prepare your garden early. Follow your local weather reports or check online to track developing weather patterns. Be ready for that first frost!

A plastic covering provides warmth and humidity, but *any* covering over frost-sensitive plants at night can save their lives during a light freeze. In a pinch, old sheets, light blankets, curtains, bags, buckets, and mixing bowls will protect plants if you remember to cover them before temperatures drop too low.

Use row covers in the spring to protect seedlings and in the fall to extend the productive life of crops. If using plastic covers in spring, remove as the season warms to avoid overheating plants, and leave the frame in place for later use.

World's Cheapest Greenhouse

The one function of a greenhouse is to allow you to start plants under controlled conditions for early growth. I've always wanted one, but I use a much cheaper alternative. A cold frame is similar to a greenhouse, only smaller around and much shorter in height. The smaller size of the cold frame makes it much easier to keep things warm inside, because there is less space to heat. You can sow seeds directly into prepared soil under the cold frame or sow in containers for later transplanting.

A cold frame is warmed by a piece of glass or heavy, clear plastic, set at a 45-degree, south-facing angle to catch the sun. This angle will collect and magnify the rays of the low spring or late-fall sun. Place a few rocks or a couple of black-painted water containers inside the cold frame to act as solar collectors. They will absorb heat during daylight hours and release it back into the cold frame at night. Make sure the sides of the cold frame are thick enough to insulate your plants from frosty night air. They don't need to conduct light, however.

MORE ▶

Build Your Own Cold Frame

Even if you go out and purchase materials to build a cold frame, it costs much less than even a tiny greenhouse. There are dozens of plans for cold frames online and in magazines and books, ranging from the simple to the sophisticated.

A cold frame made from an old window and scrap lumber

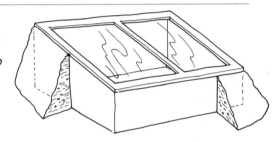

An alternative cold-frame structure made with rocks

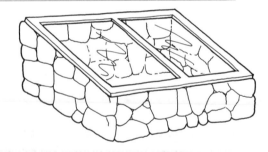

A cold frame made from baled straw

Start at the Top

First you need a lid. The size of the lid determines the size of the cold frame. An old windowpane or glass-door panel works well. A scrap-lumber frame with heavy, clear plastic stapled to both sides will work also, except during severe frost.

Frame It Up

For the frame, old landscape timbers are great, or use a thinner building material and insulate it by mounding at least 4 inches of soil against the exterior sides. Or use rock or salvaged brick, which are very efficient at storing solar energy.

Straw is a good, cheap insulator. Stack two bales at the north end of the cold frame and on each side and one at the south end. Place the lid so it touches the side bales, for as few air leaks as possible. Throw a heavy clear-plastic sheet over the top to eliminate drafts.

Put It to Use

To know when it is warm enough for transplants or winter crops to survive, place a thermometer inside to monitor when night temperatures in the cold frame are above freezing, or set a glass of distilled water in the frame — when no ice forms in the glass overnight, set out your first transplants. Start with more cold-hardy transplants, and set out more sensitive seedlings as the night temperatures rise.

Seedlings germinate best in warmer temperatures, so start them indoors and transfer to the cold frame after they develop a few sets of leaves. Once they're in the cold frame, make sure to prop open the lid on sunny days to avoid frying the tender plants.

Prepare for Winter

A major tragedy for plant lovers is waiting all winter for a cherished plant to bloom in the spring, only to find withered, brown remnants where you expected sprouting buds. One way to avoid this is to plant only cold-hardy varieties. But for those gardeners who can't resist a tender shrub or perennial, you must tuck them in for the winter.

Going Dormant

From low-lying alpines to climbing roses, many perennial plants are at risk in winter. Snow cover helps insulate plants from the dangers of freezing and thawing, but snow is not always reliable. A bad winter with freezing winds and heavy ice can damage plants that have survived less severe seasons.

Begin to toughen perennials and shrubs for winter in late fall. Nature actually does this for you; your job is not to interfere. Stop deadheading — going to seed is part of a plant's natural process of preparing for winter. And cut back on watering. This will physically toughen the plant by evacuating as much water as possible from tissues.

Over a few weeks these signals, combined with decreasing light and falling temperatures, cause the plant to become dormant. Plants that are dormant prior to a hard freeze have the best chance of survival.

A Cozy Cover-Up

The good news is that the cheapest way to protect plants is also one of the best. For tender shrubs and roses, the best protection is a 1-foot-deep mound of soil at the base of the plant. For grafted plants, including many roses, the extra dirt will protect the vulnerable union where the scion (a twig containing buds) attaches to the rootstock. The extra soil also protects the roots, which are the life center of the plant.

You can protect long canes of tender climbing roses by wrapping them with insulation. But if you protect the roots, and in most cases the graft, then the plant will survive.

Add further protection by covering outdoor plants with straw, pine needles, crumpled newspaper, or another bulky material. Wrap the plant and protective materials inside a tarp, a sheet of plastic, an old feed sack, or an old blanket. Secure this insulation with twine or tape.

Bring Them Inside

Before the first frost, dig up tender perennials, such as pelargoniums, begonias, and impatiens, and move them inside for the winter if you want to save them. To prepare them for winter storage, shake off as much dirt as possible and trim back the roots and stems. Pot the plants individually, or put them all together in one large container. Keep tender perennials in a cool but frost-free place, with plenty of light. Water only when the potting mix dries out.

CHAPTER 10

REAP BOUNTIFUL HARVESTS

After preparing the soil, planting all those seedlings, nurturing all those transplants, watering, weeding, feeding, and generally pampering your plants, not to mention maintaining all your tools and scavenging some great finds for your garden, don't you think you deserve a rest? Not yet. It's time to harvest the fruits of your labor.

Nothing Beats Homegrown Food

Finally, the payoff has arrived. With high-priced fruits and vegetables in the supermarkets and your home-grown food ripe in the garden, it's hard not to hear a little cash register ringing in your head. Unfortunately, this is where the hopes and dreams of many hardworking, cost-conscious gardeners fall apart. Either they don't bring in the entire harvest, or they don't pick food at its peak ripeness.

It's easy to get excited about the first greens of spring. And most of us manage to bring in, shell, and prepare all the early peas, which is no small feat. But by the time warm-season crops ripen, some of us begin to lose our enthusiasm. Maybe it's the food's fault for ripening all at once just when we're about to go on vacation or have company descend for a week. But it's the gardener who pays the price.

Plan Ahead

Spare yourself the guilt and expense of a wasted harvest by planning realistically when planting. Not every seed you plant will produce actual food, but most of them should. Try to project how much fresh food your family will use, based on actual grocery-store purchases of fruits and vegetables or past garden production. Then, considering the time it takes to preserve the harvest and your storage capacity, determine how much of your harvest you will be able to put up. Once you plant, consider yourself committed.

It's easy to underestimate the time and work it takes to bring a garden to harvest. What? No vacation because you have to be there to weed and water?! And it's even easier to forget that harvests must be timed according the plants' schedules, not yours. Spinach is best young and tender. Let it bolt (go to seed, which causes the leaves to turn bitter), and you've wasted time, seed, and fertilizer. Fruits and veggies have the best taste, texture, and storage potential when harvested in the early morning, so no sleeping in. Once harvesting begins, frequent picking insures the best of everything; for instance, you'll need to pick everbearing strawberries almost daily. Finally, prompt processing is a must; delay or improper processing compromises quality.

Pick at the Peak

Plants only produce fruit and vegetables for one reason — to perpetuate their species. Fruit for its own sake is not on the plant's agenda; the plant has performed its duty only when the fruit has produced seeds. At this point, however, most fruit and vegetables are no longer suitable for consumption. In other words, the harvest is not going to wait for you. It will reach its tender, tasty peak and then continue to grow toward its destiny. It's up to you to harvest at the right time.

Pick vegetables at their peak to get the most from your harvest.

Free as the Weeds

Truly free food is rare. All that garden produce is the result of an initial economic investment, then hours and hours of labor investment. Occasionally, you might be lucky enough to have a neighbor bring you a basket of excess produce or allow you to glean from an overproducing orchard, but is there really any food that just appears on its own? You betcha!

As previously stated, weeds have no place in your carefully cultivated garden, as they compete for nutrients and water. But what exactly do you consider to be a weed?

Some tolerance for those enthusiastic volunteers might be in order after all. Yes, you should still pull weeds, but as you pluck certain plants from your healthy, well-watered soil, why waste them? Many weeds when pulled young are tender, tasty, nutritious, and — best of all — free.

Of course, yummy, free, nutritious weeds can be collected beyond your garden borders, but be very careful. Never eat a weed you don't know to be safe. That means eat only weeds you know to be edible, from sources you know to be uncontaminated by chemicals; road salts; or pet, pig, or human waste. Know which parts to eat, because, as with rhubarb — with its delectable stems, topped by highly toxic leaves — not all parts of edible weeds are safe to eat. And some must be cooked to be safe to eat.

Weeds for Supper

Weed	Part to Eat	Preparation
Burdock	Root	Pickled, in soup, or stewed
Chickweed	Leaves	Fresh in salads, sandwiches
Dandelion	Young leaves	Fresh in salads, steamed, or stir fried
	Flowers	Made into wine; batter fried
Lamb's quarters	Leaves, shoots	Fresh in salads, steamed
Plantain	Leaves	Steamed; stir fried with butter and garlic
Purslane	Young stems, leaves	Fresh in salad, sautéed in olive oil with garlic and chilies
Red clover	Flowers	Fresh in salads, in soup, or teas
Shepherd's purse	Leaves	Steamed and sautéed with olive oil and garlic

Eat Fresh

The food you grow — fresh, safe, and vibrant with the energy of earth — may be the most important contribution you can make to your own well-being. Straight from the garden, most fruits and vegetables are at the peak of their antioxidant, mineral, and vitamin content, as well as rich in fiber.

But Not Necessarily Raw

Some foods actually deliver a better payoff when cooked. Cooking tomatoes improves the amount of available lycopene, a carotenoid that is beneficial in fighting cancer. Spinach and kale are rich sources of lutein, an antioxidant key to healthy eyes, skin, cervix, and breasts, and known to absorb and dissipate UV radiation. However, lutein is only readily absorbed when these veggies are cooked and, even better, when in combination with a fat source, such as olive oil or butter; likewise, the beta-carotene found in carrots.

DIRT CHEAP

The lycopene made available in tomatoes only after cooking comes at the expense of the potassium and vitamin C they contain when raw. Serving for serving, watermelon has about 40 percent more lycopene than raw tomatoes. To get the biggest bang for your buck, then, it's best to eat some of that delicious homegrown goodness raw and some cooked.

A recent Rutgers University study found that cooking improves the amount of iron people are able to absorb from most fruits and vegetables. Broccoli went from 6 to 30 percent, cabbage from 6.7 to 26.7 percent, and even peaches improved from 0.8 to 13.5 percent. But there is a trade-off. Broccoli contains substances (glucosinates) that are believed to inhibit cancer growth. Cooking it for just a few minutes reduces these by up to 59 percent.

Best Value Tips for Homegrown Produce

▶ Cook as soon after harvest and as close to serving time as possible.

▶ Steam in as small an amount of water as possible.

▶ Leave skin on whenever possible.

▶ Cook in large pieces to reduce vitamin-destroying air exposure.

▶ Cook until just tender.

Short-Term Storage

To avoid the fate of too much of a good thing going bad, it's best to know some basics of short-term storage. For most veggies the best storage temperature is between 32 and 38°F (0° and 3.3°C), in a fairly dry location. Here are some pointers for keeping your fresh fruits and veggies fresh in the fridge.

Apples. Store separately to avoid their absorbing odors. Apples give off ethylene, which speeds ripening in other produce.

Asparagus. Put in a plastic bag and use within three days.

Blackberries. See Raspberries/blackberries.

Blueberries. Don't wash before storing. Keep in a shallow container for up to four days.

Cabbage. Store whole heads in a plastic bag for up to two weeks. The longer you keep cabbage, the stronger the flavor — and aroma — become. Store a half head by sprinkling the cut side with water before sealing it in a plastic bag.

Carrots. Cut off the green tops, and store carrots in a paper bag (plastic is almost as good). They will keep for weeks, but taste and texture are best for the first week or so.

Corn. No food is less forgiving of storage than corn, though supersweet varities don't deteriorate as quickly. Use the same day as picked if possible.

Cucumbers. Homegrown cukes dehydrate faster than the waxy, store-bought kind. Store them unwashed away from other produce (they give off ethylene gas, which speeds rotting). They'll last a week or more.

Eggplant. Store in the crisper for up to one week.

Grapes. Do not wash grapes until you are ready to use them. Keep in a sealed plastic bag for several days.

Green beans. Put green beans in a plastic produce bag and refrigerate. They'll keep for about a week.

Greens. Rinse, trim off any bad spots, and dry between paper towels before storing in a plastic bag. They'll last a week but are best the first few days.

Herbs, bunched. Herbs such as cilantro, basil, and parsley keep fresh longer on the stem. Pop them into a glass of water and loosely cover with a plastic bag. They will keep for days.

Melons. Store at 45 to 50°F (7.2–10°C) in a dry place, away from other fruit. Refrigerate after cutting.

Peaches/nectarines. Keep in a paper bag at room temperature until ripe, then refrigerate up to four days. Keep away from other fruit to avoid overripening.

Pears. Pears are best picked before they are fully ripe; they will keep at room temperature for a few days. After that, refrigerate them, away from other produce. Pears will last nearly a week, depending on how ripe they are.

MORE

Short-Term Storage (continued)

Peppers. Store whole peppers at 45 to 50°F (7.2 to 10°C) in a dry place, away from fruit. Once they are cut, refrigerate.

Plums. Keep unripe plums at room temperature in a paper bag. Once ripe, refrigerate them for three to five days, away from other fruits.

Potatoes. Store in a paper, not a plastic, bag with holes in it. Keep them in a cool, dry, dark place with good ventilation. And keep them away from onions (together they produce gases that lead to spoilage of both), apples (that ethylene gas again), and direct sunlight (not only can it lead to sprouting, but direct exposure to light causes the skin to turn green, bitter, and even poisonous). Remove any spuds that start to shrivel, sprout, or rot.

Raspberries/blackberries. Do not wash these berries; store for up to two days. When preparing, mist them rather than placing under running water.

Squash. Wipe off squash, don't wash it, and store it in the refrigerator for a week or more.

Strawberries. Store in a shallow container, loosely covered with plastic in the coldest part of the refrigerator for up to three or four days.

Tomatoes. Avoid refrigerating tomatoes, as it corrupts their taste and texture. If not fully ripe, store at room temperature until ready; otherwise, keep in a cool, dry place.

Stocking the Pantry for the Winter

Let's compare the costs of different types of long-term storage. Drying or dehydrating, canning, freezing, and storing food in a root cellar vary in cost, longevity, and quality, depending on the produce. The best results usually come from a combination of methods. For instance, store carrots and potatoes in a root cellar; dehydrate fruit snacks; can fruits or green beans; and freeze broccoli, corn, and peas.

Root-Cellar Storage

This old-time method of food preservation is just as practical now as it ever was and has recently seen a resurgence of interest. It is the easiest, least expensive, and simplest way to

MORE

A well-stocked root cellar or pantry is the dirt-cheap gardener's payoff.

keep certain crops. The only downside to this type of storage in modern times is the lack of a root-cellar facility in new homes. You can use a substitute facility, with varying degrees of success with each year and each new crop. Unheated sheds, basements, crawl spaces, barns, and the undersides of stairwells may all serve as root cellars.

Thrifty and inventive gardeners have created various outdoor, makeshift root cellars. Pits in the ground or built into a bank, either natural or man-made, are among the most common outside versions of root cellars. A good tip is to line a pit or trench with wire hardware cloth to keep out winter-starved rodents. An old winter cold frame works well.

Foods Suitable for Root Cellaring

Apple	Grapefruit	Peppers
Beans, dry	Grapes	Potato
Beet	Horseradish	Pumpkin
Cabbage	Kale	Rutabaga
Carrot	Onion	Squash, winter
Cauliflower	Orange	Sweet potato
Celery	Parsnip	Tomato
Chinese cabbage	Pear	Turnip
Endive	Peas	

Preparing Your Harvest for the Root Cellar

Food preparation for root-cellar storage is minimal. The key is to store fruits and vegetables at the peak of maturity and in a cool place. For most vegetables you can follow these steps:

▶ Gently brush off as much dirt as possible, but do not wash.

▶ Cut stems back to approximately 1 inch to minimize moisture loss from within the vegetable.

▶ Cure for a few days in the sun or a warm, dry place to toughen the skin for storage.

Different fruits and vegetables have different requirements for optimum long-term storage. Some crops, such as peppers, sweet potatoes, and tomatoes, require warmer conditions than most. Other items, such as onions, dried beans, and peas, need very low humidity, while citrus needs high humidity and very cool temperatures to stay fresh. Catering to such individual requirements can be a challenge, depending on your facilities.

GREEN THUMB

Use newspaper; damp wood shavings or sawdust; dried leaves; clean, damp builders' sand; or damp peat moss to pack root crops being stored in containers. These materials hold in moisture and slow respiration by limiting the exchange of oxygen.

Store onions or garlic by hanging in old nylon stockings. Tie a knot between each individual bulb, and cut one from the bottom as needed.

Green tomatoes keep longer than those that have begun to color up. Extend the shelf life for up to four months by wrapping tomatoes individually in newspaper and keeping at 40 degrees. Darkness slows ripening.

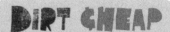

DIRT CHEAP

You can get most supplies that are necessary for root-cellar storage either free or cheap. An old refrigerator or freezer, salvaged from a dump or repair shop and buried on its back, makes a nifty in-ground storage box. Put down 4 to 6 inches of rock first for drainage, backfill around the appliance with dirt to insulate.

Place a sheet of plywood or sheet metal over the lid so that it extends over the edges to keep ice from building up on the door and freezing it shut. Mound up straw or pine needles over the top for added insulation, and keep the roof area clear of snow. (For safety, make sure you dismantle any door-locking mechanism.)

You can also bury a galvanized garbage can or metal barrel as a mini-cache. Tip it at an angle, insulate with 12 inches of straw and place a board over the upward end for easiest access.

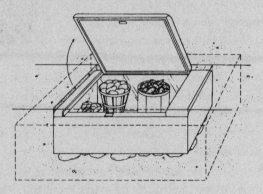

An old refrigerator makes a nifty in-ground storage box.

Dehydrating Foods

The practice of dehydrating has been used to preserve food for centuries, well before expensive dehydrators were created. Because lower temperatures are used, dehydrating preserves more nutrients than cooking or canning. Homemade dried food always tastes better and is less expensive than the freeze-dried version sold at specialty stores.

You can dehydrate almost any food. You may not like the taste or texture of some dried food, however, so experiment with small batches first. Storing dried food is inexpensive and space-efficient, and the shelf life of dried food is usually longer than that of food prepared with other methods. Moisture affects storage; a little moisture invites spoilage.

MORE

DIRT CHEAP

Dehydrating is one of the least expensive methods of food preservation available. Even if you splurge on a dehydrator, whether homemade or commercial, it will eventually pay for itself.

Preparing Foods for Dehydrating

Prepare foods for drying by first washing off any traces of dirt and then patting them until very dry. You can dry small, evenly sized produce, such as peas, beans, grapes, or apricots, whole. It's best to cut larger produce, such as apples, carrots, or onions, into uniform slices to facilitate even drying. Thin slices dry faster and generally to a crunchier consistency than thick ones, which tend to remain somewhat pliant or chewy. Slices between ⅛-inch and ⅜-inch thick dry best.

Dry fruits and herbs in their raw form. Vegetables store better if you first blanch them in water or over steam. Due to their low acid content, vegetables are prone to spoilage, and you must dry them more completely than fruit. You may wish to treat them with sulfur to hasten drying, improve color, retard spoilage, and repel insects. Sulfur is not necessary, however, and many people don't like fruit that's been treated with sulfur.

DIRT CHEAP

A friend of mine in western Oregon, where dry, sunny days are rare, uses a clever substitute for direct sunlight. She sets trays of prepared food in her car and takes advantage of the heat generated by the windows. Ventilation is not so good, but she usually gets good results. On hot summer days, a cold frame works the same way.

One of the cheapest ways to dry produce is to sun-dry it. Place prepared food on old window screens or cheesecloth frames and cover with a second layer to shield from bugs and birds. Set in the sun by day, and bring in before evening or if rain threatens.

Or you can air-dry food indoors. String up apple slices, green beans, or any other food through which you can thread a needle or string. Hang strings of food over a furnace vent; near, but not too near, a woodstove; in the attic; or near any other heat source. Space them so there is good air circulation, and drape a piece of cheesecloth over the strings to protect the food from dust and bugs.

Foods Suitable for Dehydrating

Apple	Grapes	Pepper, sweet
Apricot	Herbs	Plum
Bean, green	Onion	Potato
Beet	Parsnip	Rhubarb
Carrot	Peach	Strawberry
Cherry	Pear	Sunflower
Corn	Peas	Tomato
Garlic	Pepper, hot	

Home Canning Your Harvest

Home canning is not difficult, but can deliver a host of demons. The pH levels of food, bacteria, processing times, and proper seals are all important concerns. Also, consider the cost of jars, canners, and pressure cookers, not to mention the time you will spend. Still, canned goods are a reliable and satisfying staple in any gardener's pantry.

Different Methods for Different Foods

Fruits can be canned either raw or precooked in a liquid, such as water, syrup, or juice. Vegetables are usually canned by the hot-pack method, in which you cook them first, then pack them in the cooking water. Process most vegetables in a pressure canner. The exceptions are tomatoes, pickles, relishes, and compotes made acidic by the addition of vinegar in the recipe.

Canning is a versatile practice that can be used for virtually everything from soup to nuts. There are several different methods. For detailed instructions, consult one of the many reliable books available.

▶ **A boiling water bath** retains temperatures of at least 212°F (100°C) for the entire processing time. It works fine for canning high-acid foods such as tomatoes, pickles, relishes, jams, compotes, and other fruit preserves.

▶ **A hot water bath** of 180 to 190°F (82.2 to 87.8°C) is reliable only for high-acid fruit juices and as a finishing step to other forms of processing, such as pickling.

▶ **Pressure canning,** a much-improved process, is necessary for canning low-acid foods.

Pressure canning

Hot water bath canning

Canning How-Tos

There are vital steps to take before canning a batch of your homegrown produce. Make absolutely certain you do the following:

▶ Use a recipe based on current USDA canning guidelines *(www.usda.gov),* and follow it precisely. The techniques used in older recipes can be life-threatening.

▶ Use only premium, perfectly ripe produce.

▶ Use only new lids.

▶ Wash each jar, and check for any cracks or chips. Discard those with even the tiniest fractures.

▶ Wash lids and rings; set in a pan, and cover with boiling water until ready to use.

Freezing Foods

A freezer is not a small investment. With the ease and certainty of food preservation a freezer provides, however, you might want to consider this major purchase. The cost of freezers varies according to whether they are upright models or chest types and what special features they offer. Look for the Energy Guide label, which details the cost of running a particular model.

Tips for Low-Cost Freezer Operation

▶ Don't position the freezer near a heat source, such as a furnace.

▶ Make sure all freezer seals are tight; inspect the door gasket whenever adding to the freezer.

▶ Keep the freezer set at 0°F (–17.8°C). This will keep food safely frozen, while not running up your electric bill anymore than is necessary — such as for a sub-zero freezer.

▶ Keep the freezer at least three-quarters full. Stock up on bread at the day-old store, or fill empty spots in the freezer with ice-filled milk cartons or jugs as you use up your harvest.

▶ Only open the freezer door when you must, then close it quickly!

Preparing Fruits for the Freezer

Some fruits and vegetables freeze better than others. Some items, such as celery and greens, turn to mush when thawed. Most frozen foods change texture in some way and are often better used for cooking than eating straight from the freezer.

Dry-packed fruit is characteristically mushy when thawed, so it's better to pack fruits in apple juice or syrup before freezing. A syrup made by dissolving 1 to 3 cups of honey in 3 cups of boiling water not only sweetens fruit but also helps it maintain a firm texture.

To freeze in liquid, pack the fruit into the container, then pour cooled liquid over the fruit to cover. Crumple up a piece of plastic wrap or wax paper, and place it over the fruit to keep it from bobbing up out of the liquid, which will discolor it.

Preparing Veggies for the Freezer

Most vegetables freeze best if blanched first to retain color, flavor, and texture. Many gardeners prefer steam blanching to boiling water, because the food retains more nutrients. Vegetables should be a uniform size, cut or chopped if necessary, so they blanch and freeze evenly.

Immediately after blanching, plunge the vegetables into ice water. It takes roughly the same amount of time to properly cool food as it does to blanch it. If you just ladle them into containers, vegetables frozen without first undergoing this cooling stage turn out soggy because they don't freeze evenly. Those towards the center of the package freeze last.

Finally, drain well before packing to prevent ice from forming in the containers.

Because soaking leaches nutrients, an alternative is to drain in a colander, then place individual veggies (or cut pieces) on a cookie sheet and pop them into the freezer. This way they freeze evenly and can be put into containers after they are frozen, no rinsing required. This method takes a little more time to fish each piece out and place on a sheet, and doesn't work well for greens.

Food Suitable for Freezing

Fruits

Apple	Currant	Nectarine
Apricot	Grapes	Peach
Berries	Melons	Strawberry
Cherry	(except watermelon)	

Vegetables

Asparagus	Cauliflower	Okra
Bean, lima	Celeriac	Pea, snap
Bean, snap	Corn	Pea, snow
Broccoli	Greens	Peppers
Brussels sprouts	Leek	Squash
Carrot		Turnip

DIRT CHEAP

The least expensive freezer containers are reusable ones, no matter what they cost initially. This includes ziplock freezer bags, if handled carefully. Simply wash or rinse out, invert to dry, and store for the next season or crop.

DIRT CHEAP

Homegrown, homemade garden gifts radiate a charm all their own and hardly cost anything, since you're growing the raw materials anyway.

- **Give flowers** all year round in the form of forced bulbs, bouquets, potpourris, or dried herb and flower wreaths.

- **Arrange a food basket** with some of your abundance, and decorate the handle with some fresh or dried flowers. If baskets are scarce, make one by folding down the sides of a brown-paper grocery bag, cutting vertical slits and weaving in horizontal strips cut from a second bag.

- **Fruit-flavored spirits** are easy to make. Place berries, cut peaches, or other fruit at the bottom of a jar, fill with vodka or brandy, and let steep for about two weeks. Strain, rebottle, and decorate for a special gift.

- **Flavored oils or vinegars.** Save glass jars or bottles, sterilize, add a sprig or two of your favorite herbs (slightly crushed to release flavor) and pour in vinegar or warmed olive or canola oil. Let steep a week or two in a cool dark place and use within two months.

Make the most of your harvest by sharing it with others.

APPENDIXES

Appendix A: Recommended Disease-Resistant Varieties

Fruit	Resistant Varieties
Apple	Crimson, Florina, Freedom, Galarina, Jonafree, Liberty, Macfree, Nova-Easyro, Prima, Priscilla, Pristine, Redfree, Rezista
Blackberry	Arapaho
Blueberry	Bluecrop, Coville, Elliott
Gooseberry	Hinnomaki Red, Invicta
Grapes	Bountiful, Doreen, Hunt, Jumbo, Muscadine varieties, Scarlett, Southland, Sterling
Hardy kiwi	Issai
Melon	Ambrosia hybrid, Apollo, Athena, Bush Charleston Gray, Dixie Queen, Ediato Muskmelon, Goddess, Sweet Dream hybrid, Sweet Favorite, Sweet'n Early hybrid
Pear	Blake's Pride, Potomac, Seckel
Plum	President
Raspberry	Many varieties, including Jewell Black, Latham, Souris (*Rubus idaeus* 'Souris')
Strawberry	Allstar, Earliglow, Guardian, Sparkle, Surecrop, Tristar
Watermelon	Athens Premium, Carson, Crimson Sweet, Jamboree, Mardi Gras, Millenium, Sangria, Starbrite

RECOMMENDED DISEASE-RESISTANT VARIETIES

Vegetables	Resistant Varieties
Asparagus	Jersey Giant, Mary Washington, Purple Passion
Bean, lima	Eastland
Bean, pole	Kentucky Wonder
Bean, snap	Ambra, Derby, Dusky, Espada, Greensleeves, Tendercrop, Top Crop
Bean, wax	Carson, Gold Mine, Romano Gold, Sungold
Broccoli	Arcadia, Emperor hybrid, Everest F1, Greenbelt F1, Green Comet,
Cabbage	Blues F1, Blue Vantage, China Pride, Matsumo, Multikeeper, Vantage Point
Carrot	Bolero, Cordoba, Crème de lite
Corn	Burpee's Honeycross, Camelot (white)
Cucumber	Amira hybrid, Burpless hybrid, Carolina F1, Cobra, Daytona, Early Pride hybrid, Eureka F1, Indio, Park's All-Season Salad Bush hybrid, Sassy, Sweet Success, Thunderbird F1, Vlasstar F1, Zapata F1
Eggplant	Dusky, Vernal, Vittoria hybrid
Lettuce	Adriana, Desert Storm, Ermosa, Eruption, Esmeralda, Firecracker, Galactic, Harmony, Nevada, Ponderosa, Red Zin, Rustica
Onion	Sweet Vidalia, many red varieties, Tokyo Long White (bunching), XON 21W (white)
Peas	Green Arrow, Maestro, Sugar Bon, Sugar Snap, Sugar Snappy
Pepper	Alliance, Aristotle, Bell Boy, Golden Summer hybrid, Gypsy hybrid, Jalapeño TAM (mild), Lemon Bell, Messilla, Ole, Senorita (hot)

RECOMMENDED DISEASE-RESISTANT VARIETIES

Vegetables (continued)

Plant	Resistant Varieties
Potato*	Allegany, Elba (the most generally resistant variety), Kennebec, Rosa (late blight), and Sebago. Be sure to use certified-disease-resistant seed potatoes.
Pumpkin	Baby Bear, Iron Man F1
Spinach	Melody hybrid, Menorca, Tyee, Unipak 151
Squash	Acorn and butternut varieties, Conqueror III, Italian Harvest Hybrid, Judgement III, Park's Crookneck Improved Hybrid and Sunray (yellow), Radiant, and Wildcat (zucchini)
Tomato**	Amelia VR F1, Aztec, Beefmaster, Better Boy F1, Big Beef, Celebrity F1, Cherry Grande, Mariana, Muriel, Sebring, Sunbrite F1, Sunchief, Viva Italia hybrid

*Be sure to use certified disease-free seed potatoes.
**Look for the symbols V, F, FF, N, T, or A in the names of tomato varieties.

Turfgrass***

Plant	Resistant Varieties
Bentgrass	Northland, Waukanda
Bermuda	Tifway 419
Bluegrass	Brillian (mildew resistant) A-34, Birka, Nugget, Sydsport (often blended or mixed with perennial ryegrass)

RECOMMENDED DISEASE-RESISTANT VARIETIES

Turfgrass*** (continued)

Plant	Resistant Varieties
Buffalo grass	
Fescues	Aurora, Bighorn, Biljart, Highlight, Reliant, Scaldis, Spartan, SR3000, Waldina
Ryegrass	Derby Ensporta
Tall Fescues	Arid, Mesa, Tital and Tribute

***For best disease resistance use a blend of three or more bluegrasses and fescues for lawns.

Trees & Shrubs

Plant	Resistant Species/Varieties
Azalea	Fakir, Formosa, Indica hybrids
Bur oak	
Chinese or Lacebark Elm	
Cotoneaster (several varieties)	
Gingko	
Hackberry	
Katsura tree	
Korean dogwood	
Maple (field or hedge, Nikko, Trident)	
Pyracantha	San Jose hybrid, Shawnee hybrid
Rhododendron	Caroline, Professor Hugo de Vries, Red Head
Western catalpa	

RECOMMENDED DISEASE-RESISTANT VARIETIES

Flowers	Resistant Varieties
Coreopsis	Early Sunrise
Geranium	Tetraploid hybrids
Hollyhock	Happy Lights
Marigold	Marvel hybrids
Monarda	Fireball, Gardenview Scarlet, Jacob Kline, Marshall's Delight
Nicotiana	All varieties
Petunia	Lavender Wave, Tidal Wave
Phlox	David, Eva Cullem, Katherine, Laura, Miss Lingard, Rubymine
Roses	Rugosa species and hybrids, Knock Out roses
Zinnia	Crystal White, Oklahoma, Panorama Red, Profusion, Ruffles, Star White

America's Best

Look for the designation "AAS" when shopping seed catalogs. It stands for "All-America Selections Winner" and designates plants that have proven reliable in various conditions across the United States. The AAS motto is "Tested Nationally & Proven Locally," and its mission statement is, "To promote new garden seed varieties with superior garden performance judged in impartial trials in North America." And it has been doing just this for 75 years. For a list of all winning varieties since 1933, visit *www.all-americaselections.org*.

Appendix B: Money-Saving Vegetable Varieties

Vegetable	Varieties
Artichoke	Imperial Star
Asparagus	Jersey Giant*, Jersey Knight*, Mary Washington*†
Beans, bush	Blue Lake 47 and 274*, Greencrop, Heavyweight II, Royal Burgundy (purple), Soleil (yellow), Titan*, Unidor (yellow)*
Beans, lima	Fordhook 242 (AAS), Henderson†, King of the Garden†

†Heirloom (open-pollinated) variety
*Disease resistant

MONEY-SAVING VEGETABLE VARIETIES

Vegetable	Varieties
Beans, pole	Kentucky Blue (AAS), Kentucky Wonder†, Kentucky Wonder Wax (yellow)†, Romano Italian
Beans, shelling	Black Turtle†, Dixie Speckled Butter Pea, Great Northern†, Soldier†, (generally store-bought are cheaper than homegrown)
Beet	Cylinda†, Detroit Dark Red, Detroit Supreme (AAS), Early Wonder, Golden, Red Ace hybrid
Broccoli	Bonanza hybrid, Green Comet (AAS), Nutribud! (high in glutamine), Packman hybrid, Premium Crop (AAS),
Brussels sprouts	Bubbles hybrid, Jade Cross hybrid
Cabbage	Cairo hybrid (red), Derby Day†*, Early Jersey Wakefield†, Late Flat Dutch, Red Acre, Ruby Perfection hybrid, Stonehead (AAS)
Carrot	Danvers Half Long†, Kuroda†, Nantes Half Long, Purple Haze (AAS), Red Cored Chantenay, Sweet Treat Hybrid, Thumbelina (AAS)
Cauliflower	Amazing hybrid, Early Snowball†, Ravella, Snow Crown (AAS)
Celeriac	Brilliant
Celery	Golden Self-Blanching†, Tango Hybrid, Utah 52-70 Improved

†Heirloom (open-pollinated) variety

*Disease resistant

**SE, or Sugar Enhanced, corn is bred to mature much sweeter than "regular" sweet corn. It holds its flavor longer, both while still on the stalk and later under refrigeration.

MONEY-SAVING VEGETABLE VARIETIES

Vegetable	Varieties
Chinese cabbage	Toy Choi hybrid, Wa Wa Tsai hybrid
Corn	Bantam†; Burpee's Breeders Choice; Delectable; Early Xtra-Sweet (AAS), SE type**; Honey'N Pearl (AAS); Honey Select (AAS); Incredible hybrid; Kandy Korn hybrid; Miracle hybrid; Silver Queen hybrid; Stowells Evergreen†
Cucumber	Diva (AAS), Fanfare (AAS)*, Lemon†, Marketmore 80, Northern Pickling, Pioneer hybrid, Salad Bush (AAS)*, Snow's Fancy Pickling, Straight Eight! (AAS)
Eggplant	Black Bell, Dusky hybrid, Fairy Tale (AAS), Hansel (AAS), Louisiana Long Green!
Endive	Broadleaved Batavian, Green Curled
Garlic	Elephant, German Extra Hardy, Purple Italian Easy Peel
Kale	Dwarf Blue Curled, Red Ursa Redbore, Toscano (Nero Di Toscano), White Russian
Kohlrabi	Early White Vienna†, Grand Duke (AAS), Kolibri hybrid, Kossack hybrid
Leek	American Flag, Giant Musselburgh, King Richard, Lancelot hybrid, Lincoln
Lettuce	
Bibb/ butterhead	Buttercrunch, May Queen, Tom Thumb
Looseleaf	Grand Rapids, Green Ice, Oakleaf, Red Sails (AAS)
Romaine	Jericho, Little Caesar, Little Gem, Rouge d'Hiver, Winter Density

Vegetable	Varieties
Melons	
Asian	Canton Giant, Extra Summer Sweet Hybrid
Cantaloupe	Ambrosia, Burpee Hybrid, Hale's Best!, Hearts of Gold, Sweet Favorite (AAS)*, Sweet'n Early
Crenshaw	Early Sugar Shaw Hybrid, Lilly Hybrid
Honey Dew	Honeydew Orange Flesh†, Passport, Super Dew Hybrid
Watermelon	Bush Sugar Baby, Chris Cross, Crimson Sweet, Golden Crown (AAS), Sweet Beauty (AAS), Yellow Doll
Okra	Clemson Spineless (AAS), North and South Hybrid, Silver Queen, Star of David†
Onions	
Green	Evergreen, Feast, Parade, White Sweet Spanish
Red	Mars, Redwing
Spanish	Super Star Hybrid (AAS), White Sweet Spanish, Yellow Sweet Spanish
Sweet	Candy, Texas Supersweet, Walla Walla, Yellow Granex
Parsnip	All America, Harris
Peas	Cascadia, Green Arrow*, Maestro*, Oregon Sugar Pod II*, Super Sugar Snap

Vegetable	Varieties
Peppers, hot	Anaheim, Cayenne Long, Early Jalapeno, Hole Molé, Jalapeno M, Mariachi (AAS)
Peppers, sweet	Banana Supreme, Carmen (AAS), Crispy, Giant Marconi Hybrid (AAS), Gypsy (AAS)*, Sweet Banana (AAS)
Potatoes	Kennebec, Purple Peruvian, Red Gold, Red Pontiac, Rose Finn Apple, Superior, Yellow Finns, Yukon Gold
Pumpkin	Baby Bear (AAS)*, Ghost Rider, Orange Smoothie (AAS), Sorcerer (AAS), Triple Treat
Radish	Cheriette, Cherry Belle (AAS), Easter Egg II, French Breakfast†
Rhubarb	Canada Red, Crimson Red, MacDonald, Victoria
Rutabaga	American Purple Top, Laurentian†
Spinach	Bloomsdale Longstanding, Bordeaux, Melody, Springer
Squash, summer	Black Beauty Zucchini, Golden Scallop, Sunburst (AAS), Yellow Crookneck, Zephyr (yellow straight neck)
Squash, winter	Buttercup, Honey Bear (AAS) (acorn), Tuffy (acorn), Waltham Butternut (AAS)
Swiss chard	Bright Lights, Fordhook Giant, Perpetual

†*Heirloom (open-pollinated) variety*

*Disease resistant

**SE, or Sugar Enhanced, corn is bred to mature much sweeter than "regular" sweet corn. It holds its flavor longer, both while still on the stalk and later under refrigeration.

Vegetable	Varieties
Tomatillo	Purple†, Toma Verde
Tomatoes	
Paste	Amish Paste, Health Kick hybrid, Roma VF, Speckled Roman, Viva Italia
Snack-sized	Red Currant (*Lycopersicon pimpinellifolium*), Riesentraube, Sugar Snack, Sugary (AAS), Super Sweet 100 (cherry), Yellow Pear†
Standard	Brandywine†, Celebrity (AAS)*, Cosmonaut Volkov†, Delicious, Early Girl*, Primetime
Turnip	Purple-Top White Globe†, Tokyo Cross hybrid (AAS)

†*Heirloom (open-pollinated) variety*

**Disease resistant*

***SE, or Sugar Enhanced, corn is bred to mature much sweeter than "regular" sweet corn. It holds its flavor longer, both while still on the stalk and later under refrigeration.*

To see how Cornell University rates your favorite varieties visit http://vegvariety.cce.cornell.edu.

Appendix C:
High-Productivity Fruit Varieties

Fruit	Variety	Value	Years of Productivity
Blackberry (Combine varieties to extend harvest)	1826 Chester Hull Arapaho Silvan	High	10+
Blueberry (Must plant two cultivars for pollination)	Earliblue Bluecrop* Blueray Northland**	High	50+
Currant** (Self-fertile)	Red Lake (red) Perfection (red) Magnus (black) Raven (black)	High	15–20+
Elderberry	Native***	High	10+
Gooseberry** (Self-fertile)	Oregon Champion (green) Poorman (red) Pixwell (pink)	Medium	15–20+
Grapes	Reliant (blush) Concord (purple) Catawba (red)	High	30+
Table varieties	Edelweiss (white) Moored (red)*** Niagara (green/gold)		

*Drought resistant

**Good choice for northern gardeners

***Disease resistant

HIGH-PRODUCTIVITY FRUIT VARIETIES

Fruit	Variety	Value	Years of Productivity
Raspberry	Willamette (red) Sumner (red) 1836 (red) Heritage (fall, red) Munger Black Cap (black)	Medium	8–10
Strawberries			
Everbearing	Tillikum, Ogallala		5+
Day Neutral	Tristar, Tribute		3
Junebearing	Hood, Shuksan, Bentan		10+

*Drought resistant

**Good choice for northern gardeners

***Disease resistant

RESOURCES

Free (or at Least Cheap) Resources for Gardeners, Including Tons of Web Sites

Cooperative Extension Service Office

The Cooperative Extension Service is organized by county. To find the office in your area, look in your phone book under "[Your] County Government." It may also be listed in regular listings as "Cooperative Extension Service."

The staff is a great source of free advice on many gardening and food preparation and preservation topics. The Extension Service office can give you phone numbers for classes and programs on becoming a Master Gardener, preserving food, and composting. You can also find them by contacting:

Cooperative State Research, Education, and Extension Service

United States Department of Agriculture
Washington, D.C.
202-720-4423
www.csrees.usda.gov

State Land Grant Universities

Each state has a land grant university; these are the parent body of the Cooperative Extension Service. They offer published materials for a small fee, and you may also be able to access their libraries. (Listed under "Schools" in your local Yellow Pages.)

Cheap, Free, Wanted, or Offered Items

Craigslist
www.craigslist.com

Find Your Local Reuse Group
*http://green.yahoo.com/
earth-day/find-a-group.html*

FloridaGardener.com
*www.floridagardener.com/misc/
freegoodies.htm*

The Freecycle Network
www.freecycle.org

FreeTreesandPlants.com
www.freetreesandplants.com

Frugal Families Blog
http://frugal.families.com/blog

Killer Freebies & Deals!
www.killerfreebies.com

McGroarty Enterprises
www.freeplants.com

MyIdealGarden.com
www.myidealgarden.com

MySavings.com
*www.mysavings.com/free-stuff-
freebies-section*

Start Sampling
www.startsampling.com

TheFreeSite.com
www.thefreesite.com

Thrifty Fun
www.thriftyfun.com

Totally Free Stuff!
www.totallyfreestuff.com

U-Exchange
www.u-exchange.com

You Grow Girl
*www.yougrowgirl.com/thedirt/
2009/02/02/free-back-issues-
of-organic-gardening*

Gardening Supplies and Nurseries

CatalogMonster
www.catalogmonster.com

Fiskars Brands
www.fiskars.com

GardenHarvestSupply.com
www.gardenharvestsupply.com

Gempler's
www.gemplers.com

Henry Field's Seed & Nursery Co.
www.henryfields.com

Mailorder Gardening Association
www.mailordergardening.com

Monteran Outdoor Tips
*www.monteran.com/outdoors/
catalogs.html*

Nature Hills Nursery
www.naturehills.com

Planet Natural
www.planetnatural.com

Smith & Hawken
www.smithandhawken.com

Spring Hill Nurseries
www.springhillnursery.com

W. Atlee Burpee & Co.
www.burpee.com

Will Burrow
*www.carrilitecorrals.com/
    willburrow.shtml*
Wheelbarrow retrofit kit

Seeds and Planting Information

**International Seed Saving
Institute**
www.seedsave.org

Park Seed Co.
www.parkseed.com

Seed Savers Exchange
www.seedsavers.org
Seeds and vegetable planting
and seed saving instructions

Territorial Seed Company
www.territorialseed.com

Gardening Tips and Information

Aggie Horticulture
Texas AgriLife Extension Service
*http://aggie-horticulture.tamu.
    edu*
Information on gardening,
including pruning.

Consumer Horticulture
North Carolina Cooperative
Extension Service
www.ces.ncsu.edu/depts/hort
Information and fact sheets
on plants, insects, poisonous
plants, lawn care, and pruning
trees.

***The Frugal Gardener* eZine**
www.myfrugalgardener.com

**Maryland Cooperative Extension
Publications**
*http://extension.umd.edu/
    publications*
Publications and factsheets
on gardening, including crop
rotation

***Organic Gardening* magazine**
www.organicgardening.com

Publications and Educational Resources

Virginia Cooperative Extension
www.ext.vt.edu
Publications on crops, gardening, and landscaping; including plant diseases and mulching.

The Robinson Library
www.robinsonlibrary.com
Information on a wide breadth of topics, including grafting.

Seeds of Change
www.seedsofchange.com
Seeds and growing information.

Square Foot Gardening Foundation
www.squarefootgardening.com

Thompson & Morgan
www.thompson-morgan.com
Besides their catalog this website has lots of gardening information.

The United States National Arboretum
www.usna.usda.gov/Hardzone
Webpage about the USDA Plant Hardiness Zone Map

University of Minnesota Extension
www.extension.umn.edu/ distribution
Information on gardening and planting; includes publications on pruning trees and shrubs and grafting and budding fruit trees.

Useful Plants Nursery
www.usefulplants.org

Yankee Gardener
www.yankeegardener.com
Seeds, recipes, gardening information, and newsletter.

Composting and Mulching Information

Community Composting
Contact your local solid-waste-management agency for information on projects in your area. They may be listed in the phone book under city or town government. If you have trouble locating the right agency, call your county's Cooperative Extension Service.

Composting
www.eartheasy.com/ grow_compost.html

Cornell Waste Management Institute
http://cwmi.css.cornell.edu/ factsheets.htm
Composting information and factsheets

Mulching
Natural Resources Conservation Service
www.nrcs.usda.gov/feature/ backyard/Mulching.html

Mulching Trees
Vermont Division of Forestry
www.vtfpr.org/urban/mulching. cfm

Pesticide and Pest Control Information

Hazardous Waste Drop-Off Sites
Contact your local or state Department of Ecology hazardous-waste-management agency for information on disposal in your area.

Do It Yourself Pest Control
www.doyourownpestcontrol.com

EXTOXNET
Oregon State University
http://extoxnet.orst.edu/pips/ ghindex.html

Search and browse for pesticide information profiles.

Integrated Pest Management Program
University of Connecticut
www.hort.uconn.edu/ipm

Mercola.com
http://articles.mercola.com
Use this site to keep abreast of the current standings of pesticide residues in crops.

National Pesticide Information Center
800-858-7378
http://npic.orst.edu

Organic Garden Pest Control
No Dig Vegetable Garden
www.no-dig-vegetablegarden. com/organic-garden-pest-control.html
Lots of good gardening information too!

Pesticide Action Network Pesticide Database
www.pesticideinfo.org

Pesticides
United States Environmental Protection Agency
www.epa.gov/pesticides

Statewide Integrated Pest Management Program
University of California
www.ipm.ucdavis.edu

Soil Testing Labs and Soil Information

Agricultural Analytical Services Laboratory
Penn State University
814-863-0841
www.aasl.psu.edu

Cornell Nutrient Analysis Laboratory
Cornell University
607-255-4540
http://cnal.cals.cornell.edu

NRCS Soils
National Resources Conservation Service
http://soils.usda.gov
The "granddaddy" of all soil sites.

Soil and Plant Nutrient Laboratory
Michigan State University
517-355-0218
www.css.msu.edu/SPNL

Soil and Plant Tissue Testing Lab
University of Massachusetts, Amherst
413-545-2311
www.umass.edu/plsoils/soiltest

Soil Nutrient Analysis Laboratory
University of Connecticut
860-486-4274
http://plantscience.uconn.edu/stlab.htm
Soil tests and sample questionnaires.

Soil Quality Test Kit Guide
National Resources Conservation Service
336-370-3332
http://soils.usda.gov/sqi/assessment/test_kit.html
This booklet contains procedures for 12 on-farm soil tests, an interpretive section for each test, data recording sheets, and instructions on building the test kit.

Soil Testing Laboratories
University of Kentucky
http://soils.rs.uky.edu

Gardening Associations

Note: To search for a garden association in your area, type your city or county, and "garden association" into a search engine and pick from the results. To search for a gardening association for a particular type of plant, from asparagus to zucchini, type in the plant and the word "association" and choose from what comes up.

American Community Gardening Association
www.communitygarden.org

Biodynamic Farming and Gardening Association
www.biodynamics.com

National Gardening Association
www.garden.org

Gardening Forums Online

Join in and get your gardening questions answered for free.

ForumGarden.com
www.forumgarden.com

GardenGuides.com
http://my.gardenguides.com/ forums

GardenWeb Forums
http://forums.gardenweb.com/ forums

Gardening with The Helpful Gardener
www.helpfulgardener.com

Miscellaneous

All-American Selections
www.all-americaselections.org
You can view the complete list of winners since 1933.

Build-Rustic-Furniture.com
www.build-rustic-furniture.com
Free plans for both indoor and outdoor furniture, including a garden trellis.

Edible Landscaping
Urban Farmer
www.theurbanfarmer.ca/edible_ landscaping.html

Edible Landscaping: Plants that Are Edible
http://landscaping.about.com/ od/ediblelandscaping1

Edible Landscaping with Charlie Nardozzi
National Gardening Association
www.garden.org/ ediblelandscaping
Edible plant resource guide

Free Bench Plans
www.freebenchplans.com

Free Woodworking Plans
www.backyardspaces.com
Outdoor furniture building plans, including a garden bench.

Greenhouse Buying Guide
AFC Greenhouses
www.littlegreenhouse.com/ guide.shtml

Making Seed-Starting Pots from Newspaper
www.thriftyfun.com/ tf76607998.tip.html

NutritionData
www.nutritiondata.com
For the nutritional breakdown of all the foods you grow.

Real Foods Market
www.real-foods.net
Information on food in relation to your health.

Vegetable MD Online
Cornell University
http://vegetablemdonline.ppath. cornell.edu/Tables/TableList. htm
A complete list of disease-resistant vegetable varieties, including specific disease resistances.

INDEX

italic = illustration
bold = chart

Acid soil
   amending, 32–33, **34**
   native plant soil indicators, **28**
   plants that do well in, **30–31**
alfalfa
   activating a compost pile, 151
   mulch, 185
alkaline soil
   amending, 32–33, **34**
   native plant soil indicators, **28**
   plants that do well in, **31**
amendments to soil, 32–33, 137,
   34–35
   low-cost, 22–23
annuals, **7, 8, 12, 13 112**

Bacillus popilliae (milky spore
   disease), 163
Bacillus thuringiensis (Bt), 163
baking soda, disease prevention, 180
bark, shredded (as mulch), **185**
beneficial organisms, 169–172
   beneficial insects, **171–72**
biennials, **7, 8**
birdbath basics, *208,* 208–9
blood meal, 143
bone meal, 143
boric acid powder, 168
bug spray, 168
bulbs, 104, *104*
   cold-tolerant, **113**
   drought-tolerant, **112**
buying plants, 106–7
   when to buy organic, 116

Canning how-tos, 250–51, *251*
chili pepper powders and sprays,
   167–68

chippers and shredders, 60, *60*
claw weeders, 54
climbers and vines
   edibles, **213**
   hardwood stem cuttings, **98**
   root cuttings, **100**
   semi-hardwood stem cuttings,
     97
   softwood stem cuttings, **96**
   support system, 127
   transplanting, 136–38
   trellising, 191–93
   when to prune, **197**
cloches. *See* hot caps
coffee grounds as nitrogen source, 22
cold frame, building, 227–29, *228*
cold-hardiness zones, 9–10, **10**
cold-tolerant plants, **113,** 114
compost, 18, **149,** 154
   bins, how to make, 153, *153*
   chemical-free, 152–53
   items not to compost, 150–51
   mulch, **185**
   mushroom, 22
   saving money, 148
   tea, how to make, 146
container growing, 14–17
   formula for growing medium, 15
   recycled containers, 17
   types of containers, 16
cool-season crops, **126**
corms, 104–5
cornmeal, disease prevention, 180
cuttings, 92–100
   stem cuttings, 93–94, **96–98,**
   leaf cuttings, *95,* 95–96
   root cuttings, 99–100

Deer fencing, 175
dehydrating foods, 247–49
   preparation, 248
   suitable foods, **249**
diatomaceous earth, 125, 159
digging tools, caring for, 71–72
disease control, 155, 180
disease resistance, 110–11
dividing plants, 103

drought resistance, 111
    drought-tolerant plants, **112**

Edgers, 59
edible plants
    landscaping, 212–14
    ornamentals, **213**
    weeds, **237**

Fabric
    landscape fabric as mulch, 186
    row covers, 159
    water-permeable, 157
fast-growing plants, **45**
fencing and posts, 70
    as trellising, 192
    cheap alternative, 218
    deterring animal pests, 175–76
    hedging and climbers on fences,
        217–19
fertilizers, 18, **149**
    analysis of nutrients, 141–43
    applying nitrogen fertilizers, 21
    cost-effective, 144–45
    how much to use, 142–43
    organic *vs.* synthetic/chemical,
        140–41
    tailor-made, **143**
flowers and ornamentals
    collecting seeds, 86
    deadheading, 201
    edible, 213
    pinching to develop buds and
        blossoms, *200,* 200–1
    self-sowers, 89
    starting in containers, **127**
    suitable for direct seeding, **122**
    suitable for seed saving, **84**
    that do well in alkaline soil, **31**
food crops. *See also* fruits
    that do well in acid soil, **30**
    water requirements, 38
forks, gardening, *49,* 51
freezing foods, 252–54
    suitable foods, **254**
    low-cost freezer operation, 252

frost dates, 5, 226
frost protection, 221–29
    building a cold frame, 227–29,
        228
    building recycled row covers,
        224–25, *225*
    making hot caps, *222,* 222–23
fruits
    collecting seeds, 85
    espaliering fruit trees, 214, *214*
    freezing, 253–54, **254**
    stem cuttings, **96, 98**
    short-term storage, 240–42
    small fruits that are easy to grow,
        119
    thinning fruit on trees, 198
    with high pesticide load, 116

Garden bench options, 206–7, *207*
gardening gear, 67–68, *68*
garlic spray, 167
gifts from the garden, 255
grass clippings
    as mulch, **185**
    in compost, 149, 151
ground cover choices, 118, **118**
    edible, **213**
grow light, fluorescent, 132
growing medium for containers,
    14–15

Harvesting, 232–55
    cooked *vs.* raw foods, 238–39
    dehydrating foods, 247–49
    freezing foods, 252–54
    home canning, 250–51, *251*
    picking at peak, 235
    planned plantings, 234
    root cellars, 243–46, *246*
    short-term storage, 240–42
    weeds for supper, 236, **237**
hedges
    edible, **213**
    on fences, 217–18
herbicide, 156

herbs
  growing, 116–17
  short-term storage, 241
  sprays, 166
hoes, *49,* 52
  sharpening, 75
hoses, 63
  repair kits, 74
  soaker, *65,* 65–66
hot caps or cloches, 221–23, *222*
humus, 18–19, 40, 141

Indoor plants as air filters, 13
insects. *See also* pest control
  beneficial, 170–71, **171–72**
  repulsive plants, **178–79**

Labeling seeds, 69
landscaping, 202–19
  birdbath basics, *208,* 208–9
  edible, 212–14, **213**
  fertilizing, 145
  garden bench, 206–7, *207*
  pond installations, 210–11
  recycled accessories, 203–5
  shrubs, 119
  winter interest, 216
lawn care
  fertilizing, 145
  mower blades, sharpening, 76
  mowing correctly, 147
  push-reel mowers, 62, *62*
  sprinklers, 36, *63,* 64
  tools, 59
  water requirements, 38
layering, 101–2, *102*
leaf blowers, 62
light requirements for seeds, 131–32
loam, 2
long-lived plants, **45**
loppers, *56,* 57, 71–72

Magnesium sulfate, 33
manures, 18, 22–23
microclimates, 3–5, *5*
moisture-loving plants, 6, **8**

money-saving plant varieties, 115–17
mulch, 184–88
  money-saving options, **185–87**
  reasons to use, 184

Native plants, 109
  as soil health indicators, 28
newspaper
  as mulch, 186
  for food storage, 245
  pots, how to make, 129–30
nitrogen in soil, 20–21
  applying nitrogen fertilizers,
    20–21, 145
  coffee grounds, 22
  fertilizer analysis, 141–43
  N-P-K balance, 20–21, 143
  nitrogen-based compost, **149**
  soil amendments, **34–35**
Nosema locustae, 163
nutrients plants need, 18–21

Online research, 182

Peat moss, 18, 245
perennials, **7, 8, 12, 13, 30, 112, 113**
  planting, *135,* 135–36
  preparing a perennial bed, 136
  root cuttings, **100**
  stem cuttings, **96, 97,**
  water requirements, 38
pest control, 125, 155
  barrier methods, 158–61
  beneficial organisms, 169–72
  DIY deterrents, 176–77
  larger animals, 175–77
  repulsive plants, **177–79**
pesticides, 116
  chemical warfare, 161–62
  homemade substitutes, 164–68
  organic options, 125, 162–63
pH, 5, 24–27, 29, 32, 35
  native plants as soil indicators,
    28
  soil amendments, **34–35**
  soil tests, 26–27

photographing your garden, 183
pinching to improve flowers, *200,*
  200–1
pine needles, 151, **186**
plastic
    mulch, 187, 188
    row covers in spring, 226
pollution solutions, 11–12
    pollution-resistant plants,
      12–13
pond installations, 210–11
praying mantises, *170,* 170–72
pruners, *56,* 56–57
    caring for, 71–72, 76
pruning, 194–97
    pointers and how to, 196, *196*
    principles, 194–95
    when to prune, **197**
PVC pipes for row covers, 225, *225*
pyrethrin, 168

Rain barrel irrigation system, 43
rainfall, 5, 37
raised beds, 189–90, *190*
rakes, *49,* 53
record keeping, 182–83
root cellars, 243–46
    build your own in-ground
      storage box, 246, *246*
    foods for root cellaring, **244**
    preparing your harvest, 244–45
rooting, 99–100
    hormone, 98
rotary cultivators, 55
rototillers, 61, *61*
row covers, 159–60, 173, 226
    building recycled, 224–25, *225*

Sawdust, 23, 149, 187
    packing root crops for storage,
      245
saws, *56,* 57
seed exchange, 83
seeds, 80–91, 122–32
    best bargains, 90–91
    broadcasting *vs.* planting in

rows, 124–25
cost effectiveness, 120–21
germination enhancement,
  123, 132
light requirements, 131–32
newspaper pots, how to make,
  129–30
plants for direct seeding, **122**
preventing unwanted
  pollination, *82,* 82–83
saving your own, 80–81, **84**
self-sowers, 89
setting your seeds, 124–25
starting in containers, 127, **127**
starting supplies and kits,
  128–29
temperature requirements, 131
testing stored seeds, 87–88
shade-loving plants, 6, **8**
shovels and spades, *49,* 53
    sharpening, 75, *76*
shrubs. *See* trees/shrubs
site of the garden, 2–5, *5,* 6
soap spray, 164
soil, 1–2
    amendments, 22–23, 32–33,
      34–35, 137
    drainage, 4, 6, 37
    health indicators, 27, **28**
    humus, 18–19, 40, 141
    micronutrients, 21
    N-P-K balance, 20–21
    nitrogen, 20–21
    pH, 5, 24–27, **28,** 29, **30–31,** 32,
      34–35, 35
    preparation, 18–21
    sulfur, 21
    tests, 26, 29
    thermometers, 69
southern exposure, 2
spades. *See* shovels and spades
spreaders, 59
sprinklers, 36, *63,* 64
stem collars, 160–61

straw
  as mulch, **187**
  in compost, 148–49
sulfur in soil and fertilizers, 20, 35, 141

Temperature requirements, 5, 126, 131
  cool- and warm-season crops, **126**
thinning to increase yield, 198–99
tobacco tea, 165
tomato leaf tea, 165
tools, 47–77
  basics list, 56
  care and maintenance, 71–76
  cultivating tools, 51–55
  gas and electric-powered, 60–62, 72
  gear for comfort, 67–68, *68*
  lawn-care, 59
  planting aids, 69–70
  pocket knife, 65
  pruning, *56,* 56–57
  renting, 77
  replacing handles, 73–74
  sharpening equipment, 75–76
  shears, 65, 71–72, 76
  stainless steel, 51, 54, 57
  watering equipment, 63–66
  wheelbarrows and carts, 58
transplants
  backfill, 137
  hardening off, 133–34
  perennials, 135–36
  planting, 134
  vs. seeds, 120–21
tree pruners, 57
trees/shrubs, **7, 8, 12, 13, 30–31, 112, 113**
  pest control, 160
  root cuttings, **100**
  stem cuttings, **97, 98**
  water requirements, 38
  when to prune, **197**
trellising, 191–93

plants suitable for, 193
recycled, 205
types, 192, *193*
trimmers
  hedge, 62, *62*
  string, 61, *61*
trowels, 54
tubers, 105

Vegetables
  cost-effective plot, 115
  short-term storage, 240–42
  starting in containers, **127**
  suitable for direct seeding, **122**
  suitable for freezing, 253–54, **254**
  suitable for seed saving, **84**
  tailor-made fertilizer, **143**
  that do well in alkaline soil, **31**
  with high pesticide load, 116
vinegar for pest control, 166
vining plants. *See* climbers and vines

Warm-season crops, **126**
watering, 1–2
  automatic timers, 66, *66*
  delivery systems, 36
  drip irrigation, 42, *42,* 64–65
  equipment, 63–66
  how much plants need, 37–39
  rain barrel irrigation, 43, *43*
  stopping water loss, 40–41, *41*
weed control, 125, 156–57
weeders, 59
weeds, edible, 236, **237**
wheelbarrows and garden carts, 58
winter damage, 114
  preventing, 230–31
  toughening perennials and shrubs, 230
wood ashes, 143
wood chips or shavings, **187**
  packing root crops for storage, 245

Zones, USDA hardiness, 9–10, **10**

Other Storey Titles You Will Enjoy

The Complete Compost Gardening Guide,
by Barbara Pleasant & Deborah L. Martin.
Everything a gardener needs to know to produce the best compost, nourishment for abundant, flavorful vegetables.
320 pages. Paper.
ISBN 978-1-58017-702-3.

The Gardener's A–Z Guide to Growing Organic Food, by Tanya L. K. Denckla.
An invaluable resource for growing, harvesting, and storing 765 varieties of vegetables, fruits, herbs, and nuts.
496 pages. Paper.
ISBN 978-1-58017-370-4.

Saving Seeds, by Marc Rogers.
Plant-by-plant advice on how to select, raise, harvest, and store seeds for more than 100 vegetables and flowers commonly grown in home gardens.
192 pages. Paper.
ISBN 978-0-88266-634-1.

Secrets of Plant Propagation,
by Lewis Hill.
Expert advice on techniques to grow beautiful, bountiful, healthy plants — and save money in the process!
176 pages. Paper.
ISBN 978-0-88266-370-8.

The Vegetable Gardener's Bible,
by Edward C. Smith.
A reinvention of vegetable gardening that shows you how to have your most successful garden ever.
320 pages. Paper.
ISBN 978-1-58017-212-7.

The Veggie Gardener's Answer Book,
by Barbara W. Ellis.
Insider's tips and tricks, practical advice, and organic wisdom for vegetable growers everywhere.
432 pages. Paper.
ISBN 978-1-60342-024-2.

These and other books from Storey Publishing are available wherever quality books are sold or by calling 1-800-441-5700. Visit us at *www.storey.com*.